Answer Plans

for the MRCGP

2nd

Wyre

rv

Answer Plans for the MRCGP

2nd EDITION

Julian Kilburn

MRCGP, FRCS (A&E), DA

Newcastle-upon-Tyne

Scion

Second edition © Scion Publishing Ltd, 2004

First edition © BIOS Scientific Publishers Ltd, 2000
First published 2000 (1 85996 144 X)
Reprinted 2001
Second Edition first published by Scion Publishing Ltd, 2004 (1 904842 01 1)

Scion Publishing Limited
Bloxham Mill, Barford Road, Bloxham, Oxfordshire OX15 4FF
www.scionpublishing.com

Important Note from the Publisher
The information contained within this book was obtained by Scion Publishing Limited from sources believed by us to be reliable. However, while every effort has been made to ensure its accuracy, no responsibility for loss or injury whatsoever occasioned to any person acting or refraining from action as a result of information contained herein can be accepted by the authors or publishers.

The reader should remember that medicine is a constantly evolving science and while the authors and publishers have ensured that all dosages, applications and practices are based on current indications, there may be specific practices which differ between communities. You should always follow the guidelines laid down by the manufacturers of specific products and the relevant authorities in the country in which you are practising.

To my Mum, Dad and Robin Hood's Bay

Production Editor: Andrea Bosher.
Typeset by Servis Filmsetting Ltd, Manchester, UK.
Printed by Biddles Ltd, King's Lynn, UK

CONTENTS

ABBREVIATIONS

A&E	accident and emergency
ACE	angiotensin converting enzyme
ADHD	attention deficit hyperactivity disorder
AIDS	acquired immunodeficiency syndrome
AOM	acute otitis media
BHS	British Hypertension Society
BJGP	*British Journal of General Practice*
BM	basal metabolism
BMA	British Medical Association
BMD	bone mineral density
BMI	body mass index
BMJ	*British Medical Journal*
BNF	British National Formulary
BP	blood pressure
BTS	British Thoracic Society
CHD	coronary heart disease
COMT	catechol O-methyl transferase
COPD	chronic obstructive pulmonary disease
COX	cyclo-oxygenase
CPN	community psychiatric nurse
CT	computerized tomography
CV	cardiovascular
CXR	chest X-ray
DDS	Deputizing Doctor Service
DMSA	dimercaptosuccinic acid
DRE	digital rectal examination
DTB	*Drug and Therapeutics Bulletin*
DTP	diphtheria tetanus pertussis vaccine
DU	duodenal ulcer
DVLA	Driver and Vehicle Licensing Agency
DVT	deep venous thrombosis
EBM	*Evidence-Based Medicine*
ECG	electrocardiogram
FBC	full blood count
FEV	forced expiratory volume
FOB	faecal occult blood
GGT	gamma glutamyl transferase
GI	gastro-intestinal
GMC	General Medical Council
GMSC	General Medical Services Committee
GP	general practitioner
GPwSI	general practitioner with special interest
HDL	high-density lipoprotein
Hib	haemophilus influenza B vaccine
HIV	human immunodeficiency virus
HRT	hormone replacement therapy

IHD	ischaemic heart disease
INR	International Normalized Ratio
ISIS	International Study of Infarct Survival
IT	information technology
LBBB	left bundle branch block
LCR	ligase chain reaction
LDL	low-density lipoprotein
LFT	liver function tests
LMC	Local Medical Committee
MCV	mean cellular volume
ME	myalgic encephalomyelitis
MI	myocardial infarction
MMR	measles mumps rubella vaccine
MRC	Medical Research Council
MSU	mid-stream urine
MUPS	medically unexplained physical symptoms
NEJM	*New England Journal of Medicine*
NHS	National Health Service
NHSE	National Health Service Executive
NICE	National Institute of Clinical Excellence
NNT	number needed to treat
NRT	nicotine replacement therapy
NSAID	non-steroidal anti-inflammatory drugs
NSF	National Service Framework
PA	physician's assistant
PACT	Prescribing Analysis and Cost data
PAD	peripheral arterial disease
PCG	Primary Care Group
PCO	Primary Care Organization
PCT	Primary Care Trust
PDP	personal development plan
PHCT	Primary Health Care Team
PHR	patient-held records
PID	pelvic inflammatory disease
PMS	personal medical services
PPI	proton-pump inhibitors
PSA	prostate-specific antigen
RCGP	Royal College of General Practitioners
RCP	Royal College of Physicians
RCT	randomized controlled trial
RR	relative risk
SIGN	Scottish Intercollegiate Guidelines Network
SSRI	selective serotonin reuptake inhibitor
STD	sexually transmitted disease
TB	tuberculosis
TENS	transcutaneous electrical nerve stimulation
TOP	termination of pregnancy
U&E	urea and electrolytes
UTI	urinary tract infection
WHO	World Health Organization

PREFACE TO THE SECOND EDITION

A second edition of this book is overdue. I know this because I have missed too many of my own deadlines for delivering it. "Answer Plans" is now fully revised, updated and significantly expanded. This gives it a new position as a revision aid for those of us who think that evidence-based medicine is still quite a good idea.

The book covers written and viva questions in the broadest range of areas which have been selected to reflect current evidence and "hot topics" and phrased to test the RCGP's domains of competence.

It does not fill itself with empty sheets for writing your answer on and assumes you have access to paper. Practice exam books that provide this format claim to mimic the exam conditions but happily you will not have to write inside a textbook during the exam either.

There is often no right or wrong answer in this game and the processes you may well need to practice for the exam are those of lateral thinking and evidence-based management plans. I believe this book helps to employ both hemispheres of your brain to unlock the marks hidden in your constructs.

A word of warning though. Make sure you turn your plan into a specific answer to the question. Avoid jargon and cliché and add details to respond to the scenario you may be given. Actually identifying a few concerns relevant to the scenario may score more highly than merely saying you will 'explore concerns'.

Small variations in the phrasing of a question can put a completely different spin on a problem and require very different answers. If you are given a problem, describe your real-life approach as a GP bearing in mind the limitation of time and resources that the job imposes. So feel free to offer your response as though you do not have all the answers. Let's face it - unless you are a better man or woman than me (and I accept that is possible) – the job is such that you often will not.

In the examination room, you are your own personal brainstorming team, your own small-group without the mixed delights of coffee and conflict. Quote what evidence you can whether it be a summary of best practice or the detailed references that will help the distinction-seekers. Besides, it is always nice to try to convince the examiners you have not made the references up.

Julian Kilburn
May 2003

PREFACE TO THE FIRST EDITION

The aim of taking an exam is to pass. I state this simply because it seems to be a point of controversy with those who become our teachers and examiners. They would have the aim of an exam to be to help you explore your inner thoughts and to prepare you for a career in general practice. However, this is a happy side effect because the exam is a good one. It forces you to think widely about issues and I am convinced that it made me a better doctor. Its emphasis on communication confirms this as *the* essential discipline of modern medical practice.

Also, because of the timing of the exam, the MRCGP is an extremely inconvenient exam to fail. A retake will almost certainly seriously interfere with your immediate future plans both personal and professional and involve a different topical syllabus to some extent. That is enough about failure.

The good news is that adequate preparation combined with a suitable awareness of the game has a high chance of success and it is in this area that the MRCGP candidate wins over those taking other postgraduate exams.

The MRCGP has changed again. The exam has become "modular" and the written papers (MEQ and CRQ) have combined into one. And most importantly, the emphasis has been put heavily on the base of evidence. That means a lot of journal surfing for the worried candidate and many a happy hour at the photocopier.

The aim of this book is to present some of the newer formats of questions and answers from those resembling the old MEQ to those that request lists and summaries of evidence in a variety of styles. These are difficult to bluff and demand a familiarity with recent literature. However they are likely to be on topics that are broadly familiar to you and the evidence you quote may well be "classic" evidence that takes many years to produce and has stood the test of time.

The book provides examples of questions and answers for the problem-solving and current awareness part of the new paper one. This makes up the major part of the paper. The critical appraisal techniques are well described in other texts.

In this guide, wherever possible, I have included references of *relevant literature* to encourage the necessity of always thinking of your answers as being supported by evidence as well as opinion.

The evidence that I have decided to quote in this section is mainly in the way of major guidelines, mega-trials and major reviews plus my own personal selection of papers. Secondary references are used including those from the journal *Evidence-Based Medicine* which appraises articles found in other journals. It is by no means exhaustive but does point to some literature that you may find useful.

In this exam, any reference however vague is better than nothing. Do not be concerned with remembering the page numbers and third authors of articles. Where I have included them it is merely for you to be able to find should you so wish. It goes without saying that you will need to look up current references around the time you take the exam.

This author believes that the main hurdle in the exam is the written paper and this book is written for those who agree. Many of the available texts, although comprehensive on the issues of general practice, are of little use in the exam. At the time of writing no textbook of sample written questions and answers for the current requirements of the MRCGP exists. This is an attempt to put that right.

I have also included a section on the orals because of the difficulty in finding a useful guide and in getting useful practice. Initially I have suggested some points to consider including in your answer and then included some samples to think about and try out yourself.

Appendices have been included in a few key areas. The requirement to critically read a paper is always concerning. Using the guide at the back of the book and addressing a reasonable number of these points in your answer will turn a potential torment into a simple exercise (and easy marks) which anyone who keeps the checklist in their head can do.

A suggested list of hot topics is included. Again this is a starting point rather than a definitive guide.

Julian Kilburn
January 2000

PREFACE TO THE FIRST EDITION

APPROACH TO PAPER ONE

The written test lasts 3.5 hours and the answers can be in short note format. You may be required to give answers by entering your response into a table or similar fixed format e.g. factor on the left, comments and evidence on the right. There are typically 12 questions all of which must be answered and they are weighted equally. Questions are marked by different examiners to a marking scheme. They require self-contained answers even if this involves repetition from a previous answer.

The answer plans here do not include the critical appraisal style questions where written material is presented to you. Examples of these can be found elsewhere or practised on any article with the aid of the guide at the back of this book.

The following questions and suggested answers focus on those questions which examine your ability to solve problems and integrate evidence-based knowledge relevant to current primary health care delivery in the United Kingdom. Your answers require identification of a relevant construct or answer plan.

A familiarity with current issues is expected.

- Read the recent journals especially *BMJ* and *BJGP* of the last 2 years – note the topics that are currently popular. Be aware of the Occasional Papers of the RCGP.
- Look through other sources such as *Evidence-Based Medicine* journal, *Drug and Therapeutics Bulletin, Prescribers' Journal,* other bulletins and magazines such as *Pulse, GP* and *The Practitioner* saving interesting articles.
- A quick search through electronic databases such as the Cochrane database can identify major systematic reviews.

THE ANSWER PLAN

Success in this part of the exam depends on your ability to come up with an appropriate construct for your answer. Spend a few minutes before starting to write thinking about the structure of your answer. There is no universal format and new questions in every exam may deliberately use a slightly different approach but reading through the following pages will allow you to develop an adaptable style.

Always read the question and do as it asks. Questions that appear similar can require very different answers.

The following general format is suggested:

Introductory sentence and overview
This adds structure to the note form. A few statistics here can be a good start to creating an answer which puts the problem into perspective.

Construct: Five point plan

Try to identify about five clear areas which you can develop. Use clear under-lined headings. *This is how examiners will mark the papers. Your headings do not have to be the same as theirs but this approach will help you organize your answer and help the examiner to award you marks.*

Many but not all questions will fall into this plan and you must be pre-pared to be flexible. A mixture of question styles and answer formats are included in the book.

The use of evidence

Try and back up all your answers with some form of evidence if possible. Remember there are different levels of evidence (see Appendix 2).

The following is a suggestion of how you might use a hierarchy of evidence to help your responses.

Levels of hierarchy for exam purposes

1. Listing several references of known, referenced and balanced analysis of current thinking preferably using randomized controlled trials. Any critical comment on the references will score highly.
2. Summary of current thinking "recent evidence suggests…"
3. Quotation of specific key paper "A *BMJ* review paper last year showed …"
4. Recent news "a report recently suggested….."
5. Including some statistics in your answer.

Be as specific as possible but come the exam any indication of reading is better than nothing.

Rather than having the emphasis on quoting very detailed references, answers should reflect an understanding of the literature which allows a con-sidered personal view or a reflection of best practice. However, the sharper your reference, the smarter (and more convincing) you will look.

The *Relevant Literature* section includes references for most of the ques-tions. I have included secondary references and make no apologies for this. A *BMJ* paper that appears in *Evidence-Based Medicine* for example includes an abstract *and* a valuable independent appraisal – the best of both worlds!

I have not gone overboard on the number of them – after all that would not be a realistic answer plan. But they are all there for a reason and you might agree that some are worth a look. I will not take it personally if you do not bother.

PRACTICE QUESTIONS 1–105

1. Evaluate current evidence for the following interventions in managing osteoarthritis
• Non-pharmacological measures.
• Chondroprotective agents.
• COX 2 inhibitors.

INTRODUCTION

Symptomatic osteoarthritis, particularly of the knee and hip, is the most common cause of musculoskeletal disability in elderly people.

ANSWER PLAN

Non-pharmacological measures

Diet
- Studies have shown that obesity increases the risk of osteoarthritis of the knee in both men and women, primarily by increasing forces across the knee. Weight loss reduces symptoms as well as improving functional ability.

Education and support
- Evidence supports significant beneficial effect of education on joint pain but not on disability. The method was only around 20% as effective as non-steroidal anti-inflammatory drugs (NSAIDs), but there was some evidence for a synergistic effect.
- Formal patient education should form part of the management of osteoarthritis.
- Telephone contact from a healthcare worker can produce significant improvement in pain and functional status and reduce use of health services.

Exercise and physiotherapy
- Quadriceps strengthening and general aerobic conditioning have been clearly shown to improve pain and disability in osteoarthritis of the knee.
- Three trials of transcutaneous electrical nerve stimulation (TENS) suggest modest pain relief compared with placebo stimulation.

Occupational therapy (aids and appliances, joint protection)
- Evidence of effectiveness of walking aids and splints in clinical practice is unclear and anecdotal but they are generally accepted as useful.

Surgery
- Techniques such as arthroplasty and joint replacement reduce pain and increase mobility in advanced joint disease.

Chondroprotective agents
- Glucosamine is a well-tolerated inexpensive food supplement often taken with chondroitin, claimed to modify disease progression.
- The evidence as to whether glucosamine sulphate is capable of attenuating cartilage loss is currently limited to radiological findings which have poor validity as markers of disease progression.
- Two systematic reviews of double-blind RCTs comparing glucosamine with NSAID or placebo appeared to showed modest clinical benefit but some reservations about possible biases in the studies remained.
- Further trials are needed but current use in osteoarthritis of the knee is reasonable.

COX 2 inhibitors
- The newer cyclo-oxygenase-2 selective drugs – the coxibs – have the efficacy of traditional NSAIDs with an improved gastrointestinal profile. They also have a wider therapeutic window than the older meloxicam and etodolac so are better tolerated at higher doses.
- NICE recommends use in preference to standard NSAIDs in high-risk groups such as over 65s, those needing prolonged NSAID treatment, previous upper GI conditions and in serious co-morbidity.

RELEVANT LITERATURE

Medical management of osteoarthritis. Walker-Bone K, *et al.*, BMJ **321**: 936–940, 2000
Recent advances: Rheumatology. Madhok R, *et al.*, BMJ **321**: 882–885, 2000
Is glucosamine worth taking for osteoarthritis? DTB **40(11)**: 186–188, Nov 2002

INTRODUCTION

The GP provides the first and most frequent point of contact with health-care for children. A comprehensive service should involve special consideration of their changing needs.

FIVE POINT PLAN

Communication
- Gaining rapport helps identify needs.
- Awareness of hidden agendas.
- Important to always reassure about confidentiality.
- Lack of confidence and experience in adolescent health worsens the barriers.
- Use of child-friendly techniques e.g. use of play for younger age-groups.
- Issues of communicating with parents.
- Teenagers perceive a lack of respect and a "gulf" between doctor and patient.
- They have shorter consultations.
- About 20% are dissatisfied with GP consultation (twice the adult rate).
- Perceived "inappropriate" health promotion can cause embarrassment.

Accessibility
- Have specified children's waiting area (toys, changing area).
- Make more welcoming for all age groups.
- Open-access clinics for teenagers.
- Outreach measures at schools.
- Publicity of practice policies e.g. Internet, leaflets, posters.
- Clear policies on how to contact practice in emergency.

Practice organization
- Nominate doctor to review policies towards minors.
- Safety issues for the building.
- Written policies on seeing children.
- Training programmes for GPs in dealing with adolescents have led to substantial gains in knowledge, clinical skills, and self-perceived competency which were sustained at 12 months.

The Primary Care Team

- Consider additional training for all staff.
- Involvement of health visitor input/school nurse for medical surveillance checks and vaccination programmes.
- Appropriate provision of sexual health advice.
- Lifestyle interventions by practice nurses have shown modest short-term but encouraging changes in behaviours such as diet, exercise, smoking, and use of alcohol. Recognition of possible depression resulted in improved mental health outcomes at 3 and 12 months. Intervention was inexpensive and 97% of attenders said they would recommend it to a friend.

Confidentiality and legal framework

- Duty of confidentiality to a minor is as great as that to any other individual.
- Many adolescents fear a break in confidence from their GP.
- Awareness of the Fraser (previously Gillick) ruling.
- The well-being of the child is paramount – a child at risk of "significant harm" necessitates reporting to the social services.

RELEVANT LITERATURE

Child Friendly Primary Health Care. Hogg, C, *Action for Sick Children,* 1998
Evaluation of the effectiveness of an educational intervention for general practitioners in adolescent health care: randomised controlled trial. Sanci, L A *et al., BMJ* **320**: 224–230, 2000
Health promotion for adolescents in primary care: randomised controlled trial. Walker, A *et al., BMJ* **325**: 524, 2002

3. Julie is a 17 year old with a pregnancy of 9 weeks. She comes to you and says that she thinks she wants an abortion. How do you proceed?

INTRODUCTION

One in three pregnancies worldwide ends in termination with 150000 in Britain annually. A sensitive approach is required to minimize psychological trauma.

FIVE POINT PLAN

Patient's agenda
- Explore concerns and personal circumstances.
- Understanding of why pregnancy occurred.
- Has there been discussion with the father?
- Availability of friends and support.

Doctor's agenda
- Encouragement to bring friend, partner or relative into the consultation.
- Use of empathetic communication skills and written information.
- Need to confirm pregnancy.
- If own moral code does not allow agreement, refer to colleague (one in five GPs have a moral objection to abortion).

Information and counselling
- Guarantee confidentiality.
- Share options and alternatives e.g. continuing with pregnancy, adoption.
- Counselling may be carried out by GP or other advisory service e.g. British Pregnancy Advisory Service.
- Discuss financial help for continuing pregnancy.
- Details of termination methods and complications.
- Opportunistic care e.g. smoking advice, discuss chlamydia.
- Allow time to come to decision that she will least regret.
- Arrange review to rediscuss or fast referral to specialist.

Follow-up
- Decision on future contraception.
- Exclude complications.
- Encourage ventilation of feelings and assess for maladaption.

Wider issues
- Legal terminations are carried out after two doctors agree in accordance with the 1967 Abortion Act amended by the Human Fertilisation & Embryology Act.

- Local policy varies on the availability of termination on the NHS. Countrywide about half are done privately but there is massive regional variability.
- Government's Teenage Pregnancy Strategy aims to halve the under 18 conception rate by 2010.
- Teenage conception rates fell 3 years in a row from 1998 totalling a 9% drop.
- Evidence differs on effectiveness of primary prevention strategies. A systematic review did not show that education improved use of birth control or reduce pregnancies. Four abstinence programmes and one school based sex education programme were associated with an increase in number of pregnancies.
- General practices in the UK with female doctors, young doctors, or more nurse time had lower teenage pregnancy rates. Practices in deprived areas had higher teenage pregnancy rates.

RELEVANT LITERATURE

Association between teenage pregnancy rates and the age and sex of general practitioners: cross sectional survey in Trent 1994–7. Hippisley-Cox, J, *BMJ* **320**: 842–845, 2000.

Interventions to reduce unintended pregnancies among adolescents: systematic review of randomised controlled trials. DiCenso, A. *et al.*, *BMJ* **324**:1426, 2002.

4. Michael is a 25 year old patient of yours who was assaulted 2 weeks ago. He has not been himself since the attack and he attends with his wife who has insisted he comes to see you. What issues would you want to look at?

INTRODUCTION

Men between 16 and 29 years are most at risk for all types of violent crime except rape and domestic violence. Many complain of lack of information and understanding.

FIVE POINT PLAN

Impact on the patient
- Stages of reaction to the attack: shock and denial, fear, apathy and anger, guilt and depression, resolution or repression.
- Physical effects: insomnia, lethargy, headaches, decreased libido.
- Psychological effects: distress, depression, nightmares, loss of confidence, irritability, impaired concentration.
- Behavioural effects: increased smoking and alcohol consumption, social withdrawal.

Impact on the family
- Effect on his wife and family could compound the problem.
- Assess wife's ability to cope.
- Consider effect on his occupation and perhaps financial consequences.

Doctor's agenda
- Non-judgemental approach with appropriate reassurance.
- Detailed history.
- Make assessment of psychological status.
- Appropriate documentation of injuries and comprehensive record-keeping.
- Awareness that you may need to prepare a statement or make a court appearance.

Management options
- Discuss options for treatment and share any decision.
- Medical need for treatment e.g. physiotherapy if disability.
- Consider trauma counselling, brief psychotherapy or medication.
- Follow up for potential long-term effects of anxiety or depression, substance abuse. One study showed that levels of anxiety and depression after violent crime had not eased after 3 months emphasizing the need for prolonged support.

Other sources of help

- Advise compensation may be available through the Criminal Injuries Compensation Authority.
- Initial reporting of violence to the police may involve police surgeon.
- Victim Support offers free confidential emotional and practical assistance.
- Written information e.g. practice leaflet.

RELEVANT LITERATURE

Treating Victims of Crime – guidelines for health professionals. *Victim Support, 1995*

INTRODUCTION

There are many direct and indirect influences which restrict patients from getting access to our best care.

FIVE POINT PLAN

Physical barriers
- Location of practice and outreach clinics.
- Practice design e.g. privacy at reception.
- Practice logistics e.g. can everyone read or hear the call system?
- Child friendly areas.
- Disabled access e.g. ramps, wide doorways, parking.
- Transport for the elderly.

Organizational issues
- Updating system to more efficient computerization.
- Clinical governance and audit to maintain access to high standards of service.
- Efficient practice management.
- Financial barriers to improvements.
- Recruitment difficulty.
- Tackle motivational barriers and crisis-led work patterns.

Communication
- Use of consultation skills to permit identification of hidden problems.
- Efficient system of dialogue between all members of the team.
- Different modes of contact with patients e.g. phone surgeries.
- Training programmes for and appraisal of staff.
- Sensitivity to needs of different patient groups e.g. be accessible to teenagers, the blind.
- Encouragement for patients' advocates and representatives.

Effecting change
- Consider the principles of change (Where are we now? Where are we going? How do we get there? How do we know when we've got there?)
- Use of primary health care team meetings and liaison with PCT.
- Consultation with patient groups.
- Auditing success.

Wider issues
- Are programmes and research in place to identify areas which need improvement?
- Government plans, aims and incentives can provide pressure to make practices more accessible to all.
- Priorities and agenda of the primary care trust will influence changes.
- Role as a gatekeeper to prevent access?

6. Discuss the usefulness of the following with regards to the diagnosis and management of heart failure
   - History and examination.
   - Chest X-ray.
   - ECG.

INTRODUCTION

Chronic heart failure is a serious condition with 5-year survival rates of 25% in men and 38% in women. The majority present initially to primary care making appropriate assessment a critical step.

ANSWER PLAN

History and examination
- Symptoms have low specificity so cannot be used to confirm diagnosis.
- One study of patients on diuretics for putative heart failure showed false positive diagnosis in half.
- Treatment of symptoms e.g. with diuretics can mask diagnosis.
- Symptoms such as ankle swelling and fatigue can be difficult to interpret.
- Symptoms can be used to classify severity of heart failure once diagnosis is confirmed and to monitor effects of therapy.
- Examination: one study indicated it can be up to 70% accurate in determining cause.
- Breathlessness on exertion and orthopnoea suggest left ventricular dysfunction but prevalence of dyspnoea in the community reaches 25%.
- Best clinical indicator of systolic dysfunction is displaced apical pulse (sensitivity 66% and specificity 96%).
- Third heart sound may be useful but less specific.
- Past medical history of myocardial ischaemia/infarction and hypertension predisposes to failure.
- A study in secondary care showed if a breathless patient with a history of MI has a displaced apex then left ventricular dysfunction is almost inevitable.
- Crepitations, peripheral oedema and neck vein distension are found less frequently but have high specificity.
- Subtlety of signs and differences in experience leads to poor inter-observer agreement.

Chest X-ray (CXR)
- Guidelines recommend CXR for suspected heart failure.
- Most specific findings are cardiomegaly and pulmonary congestion.
- Cardiomegaly in symptomatic patients is highly suggestive of heart failure with 51% sensitivity.

- Normal CXR does not exclude heart failure.
- Interobserver agreement is fair to moderate.
- In secondary care, clinical and X-ray assessment of a breathless patient can be highly sensitive and specific but this cannot be extrapolated to primary care.

ECG

- Recommended by most guidelines.
- Normal ECG almost excludes left ventricular (LV) dysfunction.
- Good indicators are anterior Q waves and left bundle branch block (LBBB).
- GPs may lack skills but automated diagnosis is available.
- In one study 8% of patients with normal LV function had an abnormal ECG.
- Not reliable to confirm diagnosis of heart failure but is an indication for further investigation.
- Also confirms rhythm.

RELEVANT LITERATURE

Diagnosis of patients with chronic heart failure in primary care: usefulness of history, examination, and investigations. Khunti, K *et al.*, *BJGP* **50**(1): 50–54, 2000.

The diagnosis and drug treatment of heart failure. MeReC Briefing No. 15 Aug. 2001.

INTRODUCTION

Between 1980 and 1998, clinical obesity nearly trebled to 21% of women and 17% of men. The huge and growing burden of obesity (BMI > 30 kg/m^2) will require a mix of population-based strategies and individual care.

FIVE POINT PLAN

Government strategy
- Setting of national priorities.
- Funding of research to prevent or treat obesity.
- Guideline development for best practice.
- Tax on foods with low nutritional value and subsidies for "healthy" foods.
- Awareness campaigns.
- Reimbursement for health promotion and lifestyle interventions.
- Encourage workplace strategies.
- Health-promoting school curriculum.

Local government and community resources
- Provision of convenient venues for physical activity.
- Local public education and events to promote physical activity.
- Increase physical education in school and promote healthy eating.
- Encourage self-help, support groups and family involvement.

Media and industry
- Promotion of healthy lifestyles and realistic body images.
- Restrictions on advertisements for low nutritional value foods that target children.
- Dissemination of health information.

Role of primary care team
- Sensitive approach to a difficult area.
- Opportunistic recommendations to increase physical activity and healthy eating.
- Help to educate about the hazards of obesity and the overall health benefits of modest weight loss (5–10% of body weight).
- Development of dedicated clinics which could be combined with smoking cessation.
- Use of good clinical information systems such as a computerized registry which can track progress.
- Use of multi-disciplinary weight management team with expertise in nutrition, exercise, behaviour changing aspects, medication and surgery.

- Facilitate self-management with education, support and self-help materials.
- Facilitate a community approach.
- Develop practice guidelines.

Therapeutics and evidence
- Trade-off between potential benefits and harms of drugs must be considered.
- Lack of evidence about long-term safety of new drugs.
- Target pharmacological treatments sparingly for high-risk groups e.g. with co-morbidity.
- A report suggested that surgery for obesity is under-utilized and that eligible patients are not being referred for this potentially beneficial procedure. Surgery is the most effective and cost-effective treatment for severe obesity.
- Mixed lifestyle approaches can treat and maintain weight loss.
- But clinical trials indicate that most lost weight is regained within 5 years.

RELEVANT LITERATURE

Management of overweight and obese adults. Noël, P *et al.*, *BMJ* **325:** 757–761, 2002.

8. A 65 year old widow has been a patient of yours for several years. On visiting her one day she presents you with a gift of a new sports car and expresses her gratitude to you. How would you react?

INTRODUCTION

Gifts are not uncommon in general practice but the size of this present would raise some controversial issues.

FIVE POINT PLAN

Issues for the patient
- Are there ulterior motives?
- Is this an attempt to get "private-type" healthcare from the NHS
- Possibility of attempt at bribery.

Issues for the doctor
- Recognition of feelings of flattery and embarrassment.
- Worry that the gift is unsuitably large.
- Could be a presentation of a change in behaviour (assess mental state).
- Professional reputation – need to be seen as incorruptible.
- Acceptance may risk vilification or jealousy.
- Keep good records against accusations that could follow.
- Duty to act "in the patient's interests".

Issues for the practice
- Could this reflect badly on the practice?
- Inform partners/practice manager/receptionists.
- May need to consider removal from list.
- Review practice policy on gifts e.g. need to keep a log book.

Communication
- Show gratitude but careful explanation with patient of your concerns.
- Danger of disintegration of the doctor–patient relationship.
- Need to be firm and clear.
- Suggestion of other course of action e.g. donation to charity.

Medico-legal and ethical issues
- Ensure the patient is competent? (Gifts must not be accepted in the face of incompetence).
- Have there been other signs of disinhibited behaviour?
- Consultation with your defence union and/or GMC.
- Personal ethics – would you be happy if all your patients knew about this or if it appeared in the tabloids?

RELEVANT LITERATURE

Good Medical Practice. *General Medical Council, 1998*

INTRODUCTION

Refugees are a heterogeneous group from different countries and cultures.

ANSWER PLAN

Health problems

General

- Refugees have a wide range of backgrounds that may affect their health and nutritional state.
- One in six has a physical health problem severe enough to affect their life.
- Two thirds have experienced anxiety or depression.
- High rates of diabetes, hypertension, and coronary heart disease are found in people from Eastern Europe.
- Infections e.g. parasitic diseases, hepatitis B, HIV, TB depending on prevalence in country of origin.
- Risk of substance misuse as a coping strategy.
- Non-specific pains may have physical or emotional causes.
- Racist attacks.

Women

- Are often the most seriously affected.
- Vulnerable to physical assault, sexual harassment and rape.
- May have to take on new roles and responsibilities, including being heads of disrupted households.
- Screening and health promotion programmes tend to have a low uptake.

Children

- May be living in a fragmented family, be with unfamiliar carers, or have arrived alone.
- Physical injuries from torture, landmines or other violent trauma.
- May have developmental difficulties seeming to be mature beyond their years.
- May show anxiety, nightmares, withdrawal or hyperactivity but few need psychiatric treatment.
- Most non-specific health problems will be of mixed physical and psychological origin.
- Support for children needs to be multifaceted aiming to provide as normal a life as possible.

Barriers to care

- Cultural and language difficulties may cause difficulties in expressing needs and health authorities may lack translation services.

- Unrealistic expectations of UK healthcare and lack of knowledge in using the system.
- Lack of literacy and understanding of written materials.
- Reluctance of some practices to get involved in extremely time-consuming consultations.
- Misunderstanding about registering with a practice (it is the right of all refugees).
- Temporary registration excludes them from preventative health care to a degree.
- The effect of poverty in the UK further undermines both physical and mental health.
- Hostility and racial discrimination can result in health inequalities.
- Survivors of torture may not easily volunteer their history due to feelings of guilt, shame or mistrust.

Strategies for improvement
- Use of advocates, trained interpreters or telephone interpreting services.
- Team approach to avoid professional isolation.
- Depression is more closely linked with poor social support than with a history of torture so it is important for refugees to develop ongoing links and friendships.
- Counselling is a Western concept and may not be useful for all but can be helpful if it is culturally sensitive to the needs of ethnic minorities.
- Refugee community organizations are invaluable in supporting refugees and acting as advocates. Advice and support is available from organizations including the Medical Foundation for the Care of Victims of Torture.
- Some refugees have problems that need specialist help and support for which there are few resources especially outside London.
- Requires a change in political will and investment in sources of additional help and education.
- Patient-held records are already improving care.

RELEVANT LITERATURE

Health needs of asylum seekers and refugees. Burnett, A *BMJ* **322**: 544–547, 2001.
The health of survivors of torture and organised violence. Burnett, A *et al.*, *BMJ* **322**: 606–609, 2001.

10. Mr. Simpson is a 58 year old patient of yours who is being cared for at home by his wife of 30 years. He was diagnosed with a brain tumour 18 months ago. He is comfortable and his care package has been carefully optimized but it becomes obvious to you that he has no more than 2 weeks to live. What help can you offer in the coming months?

INTRODUCTION

A GP with a list of 2000 patients will encounter 25 deaths per year. Between the ages of 45 and 59, 8% of women will be bereaved of a spouse.

FIVE POINT PLAN

Communication issues

- Use the principles of breaking bad news to facilitate discussion involving Mrs. Simpson's perceptions and expectations.
- Use time to achieve an understanding and communicate slowly with honesty.
- Respond to her emotions and offer support.
- If possible offer a contact number to call you at home.
- Try to encourage planning for the time of death.

At death

- Attend promptly to confirm death.
- Offer practical information e.g. undertakers, registration of death, death certificate.
- Assess reaction and needs.
- Notify other caring agencies e.g. hospital consultant.
- Note in relatives' records for reference.

Initial support

- Maintain awareness that there is significant mortality in the survivor, greatest in the first 6 months.
- Praise the support and nursing care given.
- Share feelings, listen rather than talk.
- Reinforce the normality of the grief reaction (shock and denial, searching and yearning, depression and disorientation and reorganization).
- Consider anxiolytic medication.

Medium-term support

- Follow-up visit to answer any questions – this can be a period of searching.
- Feeling angry and depressed is normal.
- Monitor return to normal pattern of living.
- Allow ventilation of feelings and encourage further discussion.
- Monitor for abnormal bereavement reaction.

Follow up

- Assess need for further contact.
- After a few months grief should be starting to resolve.
- Look for clinical depression.
- Consider use of self-help group or other referral.
- Be aware of anniversaries.

RELEVANT LITERATURE

ABC of Palliative Care: Bereavement. Sheldon, F *BMJ* **316:** 456–458, 1998.
Bereavement in adult life. Parkes, C M *BMJ* **316:** 856–859,1998.

INTRODUCTION

Rationing is the inevitable reality of prioritization that bridges the gap between the needs of patients and the capacity of the health service and society to meet those needs.

General practice in its role as gatekeeper is becoming increasingly active in rationing decisions but responsibility for it is becoming more diffuse.

FIVE POINT PLAN

Levels of intervention
- **Central level:** by the government through funding, regulation of standards and clinical governance e.g. impact of NICE and NSF directives. Expansion in one area e.g. use of statins, causes rationing elsewhere.
- **Local level:** by a primary care group or practice through resource allocation and cash-limitation.
- **Individual level:** by clinical freedom of the doctor in the consultation.

Demand-led pressures
- Wants and needs fuelled by increasingly high expectations e.g. due to the pace of innovation of therapeutic developments.
- Increased consumerism and openness of complaints policies.
- Demographic changes such as increasing elderly population.

Resource-led limitations
- Decisions can be made by management or staff.
- Availability of physicians e.g. an understaffed practice reduces delivery of patient care by having too few appointments available.
- Deterrence with prescription charges and waiting lists.
- Partial or shared funding of treatments.

Information-led limitations
- Health worker education and awareness of modern options.
- Bias of communication with patients while considering an option.
- Evidence-based guidelines or clinical distillations are required.
- Patients are increasingly widely informed e.g. by Internet, to challenge the doctor's rationing.

Decision and provision
- We are progressing from reactive to proactive care, from local to national responsibility.
- Defining a limited range of services e.g. removal of NHS cosmetic surgery, dentistry, infertility treatment.

- Use of cash-limited budgets.
- Clinical governance and outcome measures can be used to explore and correct variations in care.
- New guidelines can help to ration fairly by tackling different areas e.g. education, increasing funding and resources or managing demand.
- Difficulties arise when so many GP decisions are made in a climate of ambiguity. Clear acceptable guidelines may be elusive.

RELEVANT LITERATURE

Rationing in the NHS. *RCGP Discussion Paper,* 1999.

12. What points should a practice consider in changing out-of-hours care from a practice-based rota to the use of a deputizing service?

INTRODUCTION

A more flexible approach to the delivery of out-of-hours care has been essential in the face of relentlessly increasing demands and government initiatives. Job satisfaction has increased and patient care does not seem to have suffered significantly.

FIVE POINT PLAN

Changes for the patient
- Loss of continuity of care.
- Improved care from less exhausted doctors.
- Altered prescribing levels and admission rates?
- More options available now e.g. NHS Direct, walk-in centres.

Issues for the doctors
- Cost of service and loss of income.
- Benefits in lifestyle and reduction of stress.
- Knowledge of the working practices of the available service.
- Careful consideration of alternative strategies e.g. cooperatives.

Organizational issues
- Need to monitor care provided by the deputizing service.
- Methods of measuring patient satisfaction.
- Efficient relay of information after consults.
- Need to inform patients of change to service.

Legal issues
- Ongoing obligation for 24 hour responsibility could change with the new contract.
- Legally shared responsibility for actions of a locum acting on your behalf.

Evidence points
- Those living further away tend to be less willing to travel to the doctor.
- Availability of transport is a common reason for not attending.
- Poor organization of data has led to difficulties assessing quality of out-of-hours care.
- Some studies indicate the deputizing doctors visit more and give less phone advice whereas on-call GPs prescribe less and leave patients more satisfied.
- Advantages of continuing traditional on-call rotas appear small.

RELEVANT LITERATURE

Comparison of out of hours care provided by patients' own GPs and commercial deputising services: a randomised controlled trial. I) The process of care II) The outcome of care. Cragg, D and McKinley, R *BMJ* **314:** 187–189,190–193,1997.
Out of hours work in general practice. Iliffe, S *BMJ* **303:** 1584–1586, 1991.

13. Mr. Dan Lutman is a 70 year old patient of yours who has been suffering with Alzheimer's disease for the last few years. His wife has been coping admirably with his deterioration. You visit him at home. What are the issues you consider on your visit?

INTRODUCTION

Dementia affects 5% of people over 65 years. Over half of these cases are due to Alzheimer's disease. Informal carers fulfil a huge burden of care and play a crucial part in how society cares for our elderly.

FIVE POINT PLAN

Managing the patient
- Treat any concurrent illness.
- Assess degree of problems e.g. aggression, wandering, insomnia, falls.
- Treat risk factors.
- Assess further care needs.
- Psychological status – depression responds to medication.
- Review all medication frequently for polypharmacy, side-effects and compliance.
- Role in prescribing anti-dementia drugs.
- Encourage carer to think early about the possibility of long-term residential care.

Supporting the carers
- Assess coping and offer support.
- Assess need for a break.
- Look for signs of depression.
- Open discussion of prognosis.
- Assess need for further information.
- Awareness of benefits entitlements.
- Further advice from the Alzheimer's Disease Society or local support groups.

Multidisciplinary team
- Are there sufficient local services for diagnosis and management?
- Close liaison with social services.
- Is there a designated dementia care coordinator? Is it you?
- Occupational therapy assessment to consider safety at home e.g. presence of obstacles.
- Secondary care – is there psychogeriatric input?
- Consider day care or respite care.
- Plan follow-up.

Legal/practical issues

- Suggest the making of a will and enduring power of attorney.
- Impaired driving ability requires notification to the DVLA.

Role of further therapeutics

Cholinesterase inhibitors

- Positive effects on cognitive function, global outcome and activities of daily living.
- Benefits roughly equivalent to postponing naturalistic decline by 6–12 months.
- May improve noncognitive symptoms such as psychosis and apathy. These symptoms are strongly associated with carer stress.
- Withdrawal results in a complete reversal of clinical gain.
- No clear evidence of disease modification.
- Effective in up to 50% of cases. Some patients respond well, others not at all.
- NICE recommends: That all three currently licensed drugs – donepezil (Aricept), rivastigmine (Exelon) and galantamine (Reminyl) should be available for mild–moderate Alzheimer's disease but prescribed by specialists only for selected cases.

Other drugs

These all require further evaluation.

- Statins could lower the risk of developing Alzheimer's disease by up to 79%.
- NSAID use has been associated with a strong reduction in the risk of the disease.
- Ginkgo biloba may have benefits for dementia.

14. Evaluate the following interventions with regard to improving symptoms specific to peripheral arterial disease.
- **Smoking.**
- **Exercise.**
- **Use of medication.**

INTRODUCTION

Best medical treatment for peripheral arterial disease (PAD) is both clinically effective and cost-effective. The challenge for primary care is to develop a system to deliver this highly effective evidence-based care which can reduce surgical need and prevent costly medical complications such as stroke.

EVIDENCE BASE

Smoking cessation
- The single most effective intervention.
- Heavy smokers are three times more likely to develop claudication than non-smokers.
- Cessation leads to a reduction in 10 year mortality from 54% to 18%.
- Continuing to smoke results in symptom progression and poor prognosis after surgery.
- Repeated advice, nicotine replacement, bupropion and behavioural therapy are all effective.

Exercise
- Written advice about exercise and enrolment in a supervised programme is effective.
- Walking for 20 minutes 3 times a week improves walking distance by 150%.
- Similar levels of exercise can lead to a 24% reduction in cardiovascular mortality (primary and secondary prevention).
- Doubt over the value of unsupervised exercise.

Use of medication

Anti-platelet therapy
- Aspirin 75 mg daily reduces cardiovascular events and may cause a small increase in walking distance
- Clopidogrel 75 mg daily is slightly more effective but much more expensive. The lack of cost-effectiveness limits its use.

Statins
- There is a lack of specific evidence for symptomatic improvement.
- Possible reduction of disease progression on angiogram.
- This high-risk group should all be offered lipid-lowering agents for their cardioprotective effect if nothing else.

Anti-hypertensives
- A blood pressure target of <140/85 mmHg has benefits for cardiovascular mortality.
- No clear evidence for a direct effect on PAD.
- Preference for thiazides and calcium antagonists in severe disease.
- Some evidence suggests beta blockers may trigger symptoms and these are contraindicated in severe disease.
- Avoid ACE inhibitor in severe disease due to renal artery stenosis and renal failure.

Anti-claudication drugs
- Peripheral vasodilators such as pentoxifylline and naftidrofuryl have equivocal benefit at best and exercise is a better approach.
- Cilostazol has significantly improved walking distance and foot pressures in four RCTs.

RELEVANT LITERATURE

Managing peripheral arterial disease in primary care. *DTB* **40(1): 5–8** Jan 2002.
Management of peripheral arterial disease in primary care. Burns, P *et al.*, BMJ **326:**584–58, 2003.
National Service Framework for Coronary Heart Disease. Dept. of Health, 2000.

INTRODUCTION

There has been a recent increase in demand for counselling services in general practice despite a lack of high quality evidence for its efficacy and cost-effectiveness.

FIVE POINT PLAN

Issues for the patient
- Service tends to be liked by patients.
- May avoid need for medication.

Issues for the doctor
- Awareness of available techniques e.g. active listening or non-directive listening.
- Personal need for refining own consultation skills or learning new counselling styles e.g. informative, cathartic or confrontational.
- Personal biases about usefulness of counselors.
- Somewhere to send time-consuming patients.
- Hope of reducing consultations.

Issues for the practice
- Appropriate selection of patients for counsellor will depend on his/her comfort zone and training.
- Requires available room for private use.
- No formal registration but there are recognized professional bodies which accredit counsellors.

Resource issues
- Cost of hiring counsellor.
- No clear difference in prescribing costs has been shown.
- May increase practice referral rates.
- Need to audit the benefit to the practice if going ahead with the appointment.

Evidence points
Unfortunately most of the available evidence lacks quality and many outcomes are still uncertain.

- There is some evidence that brief counselling (less than eight sessions) in patients with psychological and psychosocial problems results in better symptom levels in the short-term. Clinical significance is unclear.
- No additional advantages in the long-term.

- Unclear whether counsellors decrease secondary referrals.
- Two RCTs found no clear differences in cost-effectiveness between counselling and usual GP care.
- Systematic review of 22 trials showed no effect on consultation rates.
- High rate of satisfaction from patients and GPs.
- More impressive counsellors are more verbally active rather than just listeners.
- Insufficient evidence for the use of generic counsellors alone in major depression (though specific psychological approaches can be as effective as antidepressants).

RELEVANT LITERATURE

Effectiveness and cost effectiveness of counselling in primary care. Bower, P et al., *Cochrane Review,* Sept. 2001.
Counselling in General Practice. *DTB* **38(7):** 60–64, July 2000.
Should general practitioners refer patients with major depression to counsellors? A review of published evidence. Churchill, R *BJGP* **49:** 738–743, 1999.

INTRODUCTION

Breaking bad news is an unpleasant job for all GPs but evidence has shown that clear communication skills can make an enormous long-term impact on patient satisfaction. It has also been shown that the vast majority wants to know the diagnosis and have a say in who else gets told.

ANSWER PLAN

Several plans are possible. You may wish to modify your favourite consultation model, for example, Neighbour's 5-point plan of connect, summarize, hand over, safety-net and housekeeping. However the following points should be included.

Preparation
- Know all the facts in advance.
- Find out who the patient wants to be present.
- Ensure privacy and comfort.

Achieve understanding
- Establish patient's knowledge and views of diagnosis – "how did it all start?"
- Give a warning shot "I'm afraid it looks rather serious".
- Speak clearly avoiding jargon.

Pacing and shared control
- Is more information wanted? (If necessary, ask the patient).
- Allow pauses, silences and denial.
- Involve the patient in choosing pace and making decisions.

Respond to emotions
- Encourage ventilation of feelings and allow to cry.
- Use touch if appropriate. Conveying empathy is key to a satisfactory consultation.
- Be aware of verbal and non-verbal communication.

Respond to concerns and questions
- Narrow the information gap. Bear in mind detail will not be remembered.
- Identify his main concerns at the moment.
- Allow time and space for expression.

Summary and plan

- Summarize the ground covered.
- Have a plan for future treatment.
- Foster hope.

Closure

- Finish with positive points.
- Offer availability for further clarification perhaps with family present.
- Ensure patient has transport home.

INTRODUCTION

Nearly a quarter of a million people in England and Wales have an acute MI each year. Half die within 30 days and half of those die before reaching hospital. Thrombolytic therapy reduces mortality of MI. The sooner it is received the better. The NSF for CHD specifies a call-to-needle time within 60 minutes. The NHS Plan has given a commitment to train paramedics in providing thrombolysis.

ANSWER PLAN

Advantages of pre-hospital thrombolysis
- Speed of access.
- Proven benefit in mortality.
- Support by many hospital specialists.
- Rapid pain relief.
- Direct admission to coronary care not always possible.
- Particularly effective for rural areas.
- Recommended by NICE.
- New drugs are administered by simple bolus injection.

Disadvantages
- Require access to defibrillator.
- Needs motivated skilled GPs/paramedics.
- Special training requirements.
- Addition to already high GP workload.
- Only streptokinase currently authorized for paramedics but can use other drugs under guidance.

Evidence

For thrombolysis
ISIS–2 showed the benefit of early thrombolysis. Streptokinase reduced death from MI by 25%. The addition of aspirin reduced it by a further 25%.

For pre-hospital thrombolysis
GREAT (the Grampian Region Early Anistreplase Trial) – the most significant landmark trial of 311 patients receiving therapy a median of 139 minutes earlier than those in hospital reduced infarct size and improved left ventricular function. Mortality at 3 months was improved. It concluded that when time to reach hospital exceeds 30 minutes, thrombolysis (at least by Scottish GPs) is appropriate. Benefits do not necessarily translate to paramedics in England and Wales.

Other trials such as **EMIP** (European Myocardial Infarction Project 1993 of 5469 patients) and **MITI** (The Myocardial Infarction Triage and Intervention in Seattle) reduced call-to-needle time but were both inconclusive for benefit.

A meta-analysis (heavily influenced by GREAT) found a significant reduction on mortality of 1.6% and a relative risk (RR) reduction of 17% favouring pre-hospital thrombolysis.

For GP attitudes

Most GPs in the GREAT trial were convinced by the benefits of community thrombolysis and most would be willing to perform an ECG.

However they would require further training and considered the support of the local cardiologist important.

RELEVANT LITERATURE

Should general practitioners give thrombolytic therapy? *DTB* **32(9)**: 44, 1994.
Guidance on the use of drugs for early thrombolysis in the treatment of acute myocardial infarction. *NICE* Oct 2002.

18. **Evaluate the evidence for the following extended roles in primary care.**
  ● **Consultation of patients with a nurse practitioner.**
  ● **The community pharmacist and practice prescribing.**

INTRODUCTION

With Pharmacy in the Future, the government is committed to an increased role for the pharmacist. Both pharmacists and nurse practitioners treat minor illness.

Nurse practitioners

- Much research is of dubious quality and conducted on experienced volunteers rather than the variably skilled and motivated.
- Appear to be a safe alternative to GPs for minor illness.
- Less productive i.e. longer consultations and more investigations.
- Some claims of increased patient satisfaction probably related to consultation length.
- No clear differences found in number of prescriptions, need for further consultations, or referrals.
- The extra time and investigation may show an inability to diagnose conditions.
- Concern has been expressed about ability to find rare but important health problems.
- A systematic review (below) concluded that patients are more satisfied with care from a nurse practitioner than from a doctor. However this trial admitted to including hospital practitioners in their study and the ambiguity of the definition of the role has been pointed out. The research was done on same day appointments for minor illness – a small part of GP workload. And also on a self-triaging group who were willing to see a nurse practitioner.

Role for the community pharmacist

- Studies have suggested that in elderly patients, a pharmacist review of repeat prescriptions can result in more prescription changes, fewer medications prescribed and lower medication costs than usual GP review. More than the cost of the intervention was saved without affecting GP workload.
- A study of over 3000 patients in 19 practices involved 62 pharmacists working to a protocol. Compliance problems, side effects, adverse reactions and interactions were identified in 12%. Substantial savings could be made through reduction of medication. Clinical problems were highlighted and feasibility of the approach was demonstrated.
- Electronic transfer of prescriptions to the pharmacist appears to be acceptable to patients, doctors and pharmacists. Some concern has been expressed about maintenance of confidentiality of the medical record with such systems.

RELEVANT LITERATURE

Randomised controlled trial of nurse practitioner versus general practitioner care for patients requesting "same day" consultations in primary care. Venning, P et al., BMJ **320:** 1043–1048, 2000.

Systematic review of whether nurse practitioners working in primary care can provide equivalent care to doctors. Horrocks, S et al., BMJ **324:** 819–823, 2002.

Pharmacy in the Future: Implementing the NHS Plan – a programme for pharmacy in the National Health Service. Dept of Health, 2000.

Repeat prescribing: a role for community pharmacists in controlling and monitoring repeat prescriptions. Bond, C et al., BJGP **50(4):** 271–275, 2000.

Electronic transfer of prescription-related information: comparing views of patients, general practitioners, and pharmacists. Porteous, T et al., BJGP **53(3):** 204–209, 2003.

Pharmacist review changed more repeat prescriptions for elderly patients than usual general practice review. EBM **7:** 158, 2002.

INTRODUCTION

In most cases, the condition is minor and self-limiting and may not present to the GP but a significant number get unacceptable morbidity, loss of earnings etc. Antibiotics of questionable efficacy are therefore often handed out by GPs.

EVIDENCE

Presentation
- Clinical examination is unreliable for differentiating between viral and bacterial infection. It lacks sufficient sensitivity and specificity.
- Studies on the predictive value of constellations of symptoms are conflicting and inconclusive.
- Practitioners should be aware of underlying psychosocial influences in patients presenting with sore throat.
- Studies show that GPs often perceive more pressure to prescribe than actually exists.

Diagnosis
Common testing methods include throat swab and rapid antigen testing. Anti-streptolysin O titre is a gold standard for research but with no practical clinical value.

Throat swab culture
- Should not be carried out routinely in sore throat.
- Are not cost-effective (cost £4 and report takes 24–48 hours).
- Detect carriage as well as infection.
- Negative culture does not rule out streptococcal infection.
- Can medicalize illness.

Rapid Antigen Testing (near patient testing)
- Should not be carried out routinely in sore throat.
- Costs £4 and takes 10 minutes to report.
- Sensitivity varies between 61% and 95%
- Use of the test changes prescribing patterns very little.

Treatment

Analgesics
- Paracetamol is appropriate for all ages.
- Ibuprofen also has proven effectiveness.

Education

- Patient information leaflets may empower home management in future.

Antibiotics

Should not be withheld in serious cases of concern but evidence does not support routine use to:

- reduce symptoms;
- prevent rheumatic fever or glomerulonephritis;
- prevent cross infection in the general community;
- prevent suppurative complications.

Benefits of antibiotics are marginal but include:

- reduces short-term symptoms by about 16 hours. Effect maximal at day 3–4;
- reduced risk of rheumatic fever by 30% but benefits not clinically relevant in the UK;
- reduced suppurative complications such as otitis media, sinusitis, mastoiditis and quinsy.

Marginal benefit of antibiotics tends not to be translated into cost-effectiveness.

Cochrane review concludes the modest absolute benefits can only be achieved by treating many with antibiotics who will derive no benefit.

Side effects include anaphylaxis and death, candidiasis, diarrhoea and unwanted pregnancy.

Ampicillin-based antibiotics should be avoided first line due to chance of infectious mononucleosis.

The preferred regime when treating (suspected) Group A β-haemolytic streptococcus is 10 day course of penicillin q.d.s. which may reduce recurrence.

Prescribing has been shown to increase reattendance.

RELEVANT LITERATURE

Management of sore throat and indications for tonsillectomy. *SIGN Guideline No 34*, www.sign.ac.uk.
Diagnosis and treatment of streptococcal sore throat. *DTB* 33(2): 9–11, 1995.
Antibiotics for sore throat. Del Mar, C B *et al.*, *Cochrane Review*, 2000.
Antibiotic prescribing and admissions with major suppurative complications of respiratory tract infections: a data linkage study. Little, P *et al.*, *BJGP* 52(3): 187–195, 2002.

INTRODUCTION

Difficulty achieving a pregnancy is a common problem with around one in five couples reporting problems. Fertility drops off with age. Infertility is defined as pregnancy not occurring after 12 months of regular unprotected intercourse.

FIVE POINT PLAN

Patient-related issues
- Develop and understand her expectations and concerns.
- Nature and stability of her relationship with younger partner.
- Do both partners have a mutual desire for this?

Self-awareness of the doctor
- Time consuming and complex consultation.
- After only 3 months probably no need for immediate action.
- Possible awkwardness for male doctor depending on expertise and personal experience.
- Knowledge of secondary care techniques and current local success levels.

Consultation issues
- Need to develop rapport and understanding.
- It takes two to be infertile – preferable to see both partners together and separately.
- Context of known previous consultations.
- May be able to be reassuring at this stage and give lifestyle advice and encourage patience.
- Explanation of how you might proceed if situation does not change e.g. blood tests, referral.
- Agree review date to continue process perhaps with partner next time.
- Opportunity for preconceptual advice e.g. use of folate.

Clinical aspects
- Full medical, menstrual and sexual history for the couple.
- Has either partner been involved in a successful pregnancy?
- Inquire about medication, smoking and alcohol.
- Are there local protocols?
- Relevant aspects of examination e.g. to exclude need for prompt referral.
- Is there a need to refer earlier rather than later in view of her age?

Wider issues

- Expense of assisted fertilization if needed.
- Availability of local resources and awareness of protocols.
- Are there counselling and support groups available?
- Future role of GP in care team e.g. prescribing and administering drugs for assisted conception.
- Long-term support from primary care may be needed if going down this route.
- What should be the obligations of NHS in this area?

INTRODUCTION

Part of the NHS Plan includes a new model that includes an intermediate level specialist – the GPwSI – in primary care This aims to deliver a high quality, improved access service to meet the needs of a single PCT or group of PCTs.

Already 16% of GPs in the UK provide specialist clinical services outside their core general practice commitments.

FOUR POINT PLAN

Issues for the doctor
- A new role with opportunity for personal development.
- New skills help prevent burnout.
- Need to ensure clinical governance.
- Will need to maintain a PDP which includes audit and annual appraisal.
- Requires additional training and should be on a national register.
- May lose generalist focus.

Issues for patient care
- Quicker access at a location close to the patient.
- Need to avoid becoming a barrier to true consultant appointments for appropriate cases.
- Service should support the wider primary health community.
- Patient education needed to clarify role.

Practice issues
- Other partners have to cover more standard work – may lead to friction.
- Increased burden on practice administrative staff if using own premises.
- Should foster closer relations between practices and with local hospitals.
- Danger of fragmentation of general practice.

Organizational aspects
- Need to identify local health needs and gather support from secondary care and other primary care colleagues.
- Clinics run independently but will need occasional supervision from a willing local consultant.
- GP is accountable to the PCT and may take referrals from a large area.

- Need to discuss indemnity with defence union and inform PCT of arrangements.
- Appropriate remuneration.
- Need to obtain funding for training and equipment.
- Need direct access to secondary investigations and own prescribing budget.

RELEVANT LITERATURE

General practitioners with a special clinical interest: a model for improving respiratory disease management. Williams, S *et al.*, *BJGP* **52(10)**: 838–943, 2002.
General practitioners with special clinical interests: a cross-sectional survey. Jones, R *et al.*, *BJGP* **52(10)**: 833–834, 2002.

22. Comment on the evidence for the following.
- Lifestyle factors for preventing fracture.
- Treatment of osteoporosis in men.

INTRODUCTION

Osteoporosis affects one in three women and one in 12 men and results in over 200 000 fractures per year. Approximately 30% of people over 65 years of age and living in the community (and more in institutions) fall each year. Although less than one fall in 10 results in a fracture, a fifth of fall incidents require medical attention.

EVIDENCE BASE

Lifestyle advice
- Best targeted at at-risk individuals e.g. previous fragility fractures, maternal history of hip fracture, low BMI, early menopause and corticosteroid treatment.
- Balanced diet with adequate calcium intake and sun exposure (less than 15 min per day for half the year).
- Calcium and Vitamin D supplements in the institutionalised frail elderly are a reasonable option as requirements can be higher than usual in this age group.
- Moderation of alcohol consumption.
- Weight-bearing exercise is effective at preserving bone mass but also increases mobility and confidence in the elderly which is beneficial.
- Hip protectors appear to reduce hip fracture in high-risk individuals. They are available on the NHS but can be bulky and uncomfortable.
- Quitting smoking appears to reduce fracture risk and should be encouraged.
- Fall prevention programmes which tackle hazards at home, medication review and mobility issues can reduce fracture by 20–50%. Risks in this group include visual impairment, impaired cognition, postural hypotension, poor lighting, steep stairs etc.

Osteoporosis in men
- An important issue – up to 30% of hip fractures occur in this group.
- Limited evidence for best drug as most research has been done on women.
- The Royal College of Physicians recommends early referral to specialist centre for thorough investigation particularly if under 65.
- Additional underlying causes such as hypogonadism may require treatment. Testosterone may also be of value in some eugonadal men with vertebral osteoporosis.
- Some RCT evidence supports use of bisphophonates (etidronate and elandronate) in men.

- Strongest evidence is in favour of alendronate reducing vertebral fracture over 2 years.
- Men over 65 years may benefit from a calcium and Vitamin D supplement to increase BMD.
- Regular vitamin D supplements alone can reduce fractures in the community by 22% and 33% in major sites.
- Human parathyroid hormone has also shown promise in reducing fractures.
- Calcitriol has been studied but not yet shown positive effects.
- Treatment should be reviewed with repeat dual energy X-ray absorptiometry to identify non-responders.
- Treatment protocols remain to be clearly established.

RELEVANT LITERATURE

Osteoporosis – Clinical Guidelines for the Prevention and Treatment. *Royal College of Physicians,* London,1999.
Lifestyle advice for fracture prevention. *DTB* **40(11):** 89–91, Nov 2002.
Interventions for preventing falls in elderly people (Cochrane Review). *The Cochrane Library,* Issue 4, 2002.
National Service Framework for Older People. *Dept of Health,* March 2001, London.
Osteoporosis. Tuck, S P *et al., Postgrad. Med. J.* **78:** 526–32, 2000.
Effect of four monthly oral vitamin D3 (cholecalciferol) supplementation on fractures and mortality in men and women living in the community: randomised double blind controlled trial. Trivedi, D P *et al., BMJ* **326:** 469, 2003.

INTRODUCTION

Single-handed GPs tend to work in areas of high deprivation and need. Concerns have been expressed about professional isolation and quality standards for single-handed practice, on the basis of little evidence. However numbers are dropping.

ANSWER PLAN

- Patients like single-handed practices because of good communication, personal rapport, availability, and continuity of care. While patients rate this, its existence is under threat.
- Levels of patient satisfaction fall in practices with bigger lists and in particular no personal lists.
- Some research suggests reduced usage of guidelines and audit in smaller practices.
- A study of 60 general practices in England measured quality in many areas. Quality of clinical care varied substantially, and access to care, continuity of care, and interpersonal care varied moderately. Scores for asthma, diabetes, and angina were better in practices with longer booking intervals. Diabetes care was better in larger practices but access to care was better in small practices. The report concluded that no single type of practice has a monopoly on high quality care and that different types of practice may have different strengths.
- In another study, most aspects of the management of ischaemic heart disease in primary care were not associated with the number of cases managed. No association between practice size and the quality of care was demonstrated suggesting that the trend in the NHS towards larger general practices by itself has little impact on the quality of chronic disease management in primary care.
- A study of 206 single-handed practices and 606 partnerships in the UK failed to demonstrate differences in achievement of immunization and cytology targets or in hospital admissions after adjustment for other practice characteristics.
- Evidence generally does not support solo GPs underperforming clinically.
- Other practice characteristics such as deprived areas and ethnic demography seem of much more importance. These factors may cause solo GPs to have lower achievement of targets.

RELEVANT LITERATURE

Do single handed practices offer poorer care? Cross sectional survey of processes and outcomes. Hippisley-Cox, J. *BMJ* **323:** 320–323, 2001.

Association between practice size and quality of care of patients with ischaemic heart disease: cross sectional study. Majeed, A *et al.*, *BMJ* **326:** 371–372 , 2003.

Identifying predictors of high quality care in English general practice: observational study. Campbell, S M *et al.*, *BMJ* **323:** 784, 2001.

INTRODUCTION

Before primary care comes self-care. Numerous products are available over the counter such as BP equipment and kits to test for glycosuria and cholesterol. Internet sites market tests for UTI, HIV, malaria, hepatitis C, Alzheimer's and osteoporosis.

ANSWER PLAN

Pros
- Can detect potential disease.
- Rapid result, earlier treatment.
- Perception of instant answers.
- Patient satisfaction – fulfils a clinical need.
- Sign of active interest and personal responsibility for own health care.
- Opportunity to recruit patient in helping monitor own care e.g. BMs.
- Opportunity for testing at otherwise inconvenient times of day.
- Negative result may reassure.
- Educates patient e.g. fertility tests leading to more understanding of cycle.
- Empowers patient e.g. able to perform own INRs and avoid attending clinics.
- Same technological developments can be used by GPs for point of care testing e.g. use of Coaguchek in anticoagulation clinics.
- Future possibilities e.g. use of cardiac markers.

Cons
- Evades any chance for pre-test counselling.
- Positives or false positives create huge anxiety.
- May be used to condone an unhealthy approach to lifestyle.
- Often tests are not validated tests for screening.
- Need to read instructions and act on them.
- Potential for misreading.
- Interpretation is the most important thing.
- Patients need tests in context with medical history/examination.
- Expensive (but devolves cost to the patient!) – a type of rationing.
- Panders to hypochondria (cf "quick doctor, measure my blood pressure").
- Extra workload for GP dealing with the consequences.
- Need for full reassessment and retesting with investigations of appropriate sensitivity.
- Lacks research on cost-benefit analysis.

RELEVANT LITERATURE

Point of care testing. Price, C P *BMJ* **322:** 1285–1288, 2001.

25. A 55 year old man comes to your surgery after his recent admission for acute MI. You discover he has not taken any medication since his hospital prescription ran out 7 days after discharge. No discharge letter is available. List the three main types of drug you would expect him to be on as a result of his MI supporting your answer with evidence.

INTRODUCTION

Many large well-conducted studies have supported the role of aspirin, beta-blockers and ACE inhibitors after MI. Patients may also need treatments for co-existing conditions such as hypertension and hyperlipidaemia at lower thresholds than for primary prevention.

ANSWER PLAN

Antiplatelets
- The ISIS–2 trial proved for every 1000 patients treated, aspirin prevented 38 fatal and non-fatal vascular events including MI, stroke and death.
- Meta-analysis by the Antiplatelet Trialists Collaboration (1994) showed lower mortality and reinfarction rates by 25%.
- It is the most cost-effective agent.
- 75–150 mg/day indefinitely for all patients unless contraindicated.
- Aspirin alone has been shown to be as effective as the combination of aspirin and dipyridamole.
- Clopidogrel (75 mg/day) is an effective alternative in patients with contraindications or intolerance to aspirin.

Beta blockers
- The ISIS 1 trial illustrated post-MI benefit.
- The Norwegian Multicentre Study using timolol resulted in a 39% reduction in overall mortality and a 28% reduction in re-infarction at 33 months with an absolute risk reduction of 4.6%.
- Meta-analysis of 25 randomized trials involving over 20 000 patients on long term beta-blocker therapy after MI showed a 23% reduction in total mortality (NNT = 51) and a 32% reduction in sudden death (presumably an antiarrhythmic effect).
- Continue indefinitely if not contraindicated e.g. respiratory disease, uncontrolled heart failure.

ACE inhibitors
- SAVE trial (Survival and Ventricular Enlargement) – 2231 patients with low ejection fraction (< 40%) but no signs of heart failure were given captopril post-MI. All-cause mortality was reduced by 19% over 3.5 years corresponding to an absolute risk reduction of 4.2% (NNT over 42 months = 24).

- In the Acute Infarction Ramipril Efficacy (AIRE) study in patients with clinical evidence of heart failure post-infarction, the ramipril group had significant reductions of 27% in mortality and 19% in a combined CV endpoints (ARR 5.6%, NNT over 15 months = 22). Extension to the AIRE Study (AIREX) found that the use of ramipril for 1 year provided continuing mortality benefit for up to 6 years.
- The ISIS 4 trial of nearly 60 000 patients treated with captopril also showed persisting reduction in mortality post-MI as well as a 7% mortality reduction at 35 days.
- Long term ACE inhibitor therapy should be considered for all patients following MI with or without left ventricular dysfunction, unless there are contraindications.
- Greatest benefit in those with LV dysfunction and those who develop early heart failure.

RELEVANT LITERATURE

Secondary Prevention of Coronary Heart Disease following Myocardial Infarction. *SIGN Guideline No. 41.*

INTRODUCTION

Men are a difficult proposition. They attend their GP half as often as women and present late with more advanced illness. Men have higher mortality rates for all 15 leading causes of death and a life expectancy about 7 years shorter than women's. Palatable health initiatives are needed to bridge the gap.

ANSWER PLAN

Barriers

- **Concern.** Men do worry about health but are less likely to talk about their problems with their peers or health professionals.
- **Knowledge** of health matters is often poor. In one survey, 18% of men thought a GUM clinic dealt with dental problems. Lack of awareness contributes to late diagnosis and poor outcome.
- **Media.** Less likely than women to seek advice from magazines, books, and TV. Girls have numerous such magazines – boys wait till they are old enough for Loaded.
- **Social class.** Lower class men less likely to present or respond to health promotion measures.
- **Personality.** Strength through silence, bravado, especially in young men.
- **Perception.** Health care held by many men from an early age to be the domain of women e.g. boys tend to be brought to the doctor by mother.
- **Education.** Health studies a low priority in schools.
- **Practice barriers.** Perceived as male-unfriendly with few male receptionists or nurses, causing danger of embarrassment.
- **Doctor barriers.** Men receive significantly less time in medical encounters than women, get fewer and briefer explanations, and receive less opportunistic advice about changing risk factors.
- **Well-man clinics** are nowhere near as ubiquitous as well-woman clinics.
- **Lack of any government initiative** on general male health screening
- **Lack of printed information**. Virtually no health promotion literature is produced for men other than on sexual health.

Interventions

Education

- Requires a fundamental change in school education.
- Uptake of health information and health services can be improved by making them male-friendly, anonymous, and more convenient.
- Change emphasis in training of health professionals e.g. in medical school.

Occupational health
- Improved use of occupational health services for health promotion.

Development of a well-man clinic
- Decide what to target e.g. smoking, alcohol, cholesterol, BP.
- Screening issues – discuss pros and cons of testicular self-examination, FOBs in the over 50s, PSA test in men with outflow obstruction.
- Nominate team, select approach, methods and interventions e.g. CAGE questionnaire, brief anti-smoking advice.
- Practice issues e.g. training courses for staff, cost, use of registers.
- Review and audit – to assess success and popularity.
- Incorporate changes in national advice and future guidelines e.g. from the National Screening Programme.

New initiatives
- Recent government initiatives include NHS Direct, NHS Direct Online, walk-in primary care centres. Gender issues should influence all future policies.
- NHS Direct Online is used equally by both sexes.
- Anonymous telephone helplines have been shown to be very useful for erectile dysfunction. Role could be expanded.

RELEVANT LITERATURE

No man's land: men, illness, and the NHS. Banks, I. *BMJ* **323:** 1058, 2001.

INTRODUCTION

As part of the developments in primary care, closer bonds with other health professionals are being established.

ANSWER PLAN

Role of pharmacists in the community
- Unique access to healthy people helps promotion of health.
- Often the first port of call for patients.
- Education of patients about medication.
- Facilitate responsible self-medication.
- Prepare monitored dosage regimens.
- Can provide support to patients in their homes.
- Provide collection and delivery services.
- Can provide a "medicines assessment service".
- Health promotion activities in schools etc.
- Proposed pharmacy deregulation will put small pharmacies up against the big supermarkets in the expectations that competition will reduce cost.

Role for the practice
- Could reduce the frequency of GP consultation.
- Promote efficient and cost-effective prescribing.
- Rationalize repeat prescription system.
- Benefits can offset employment costs.
- Help create a practice formulary.
- Already have experience of working towards defined business targets.
- Potential to improve patient compliance with treatment.
- Address patient concerns not voiced to the doctor.
- Relay information about patient's view of their treatment e.g. drugs returned to the pharmacy.
- Improved medicine management may reduce admission rates.
- Deregulation could make pharmacy ownership by large practices viable.

Role in primary care groups
- Have knowledge and skills to allow many varied roles.
- Local Pharmaceutical Committees (LPCs) can help primary care groups to achieve objectives.

INTRODUCTION

Evidence has shown a high satisfaction for the type of work of general practice but this drops sharply when stress is perceived in personal and work-related areas. Stress is high in young idealists and patient-centred GPs.

ANSWER PLAN

Recognize causes

Personal
- High expectations from patients.
- High expectations of self.
- Fear of complaints and litigation.
- Personality clashes with colleagues.
- Reduced autonomy.
- Lack of training and experience.
- Interference with family life.

Professional
- Case-mix e.g. working in a deprived area.
- Constant interruptions at work e.g. phone.
- Ever-increasing workload.
- New contracts and regulations.
- Effect of professional isolation.

Finding solutions

Personal
- Accept the unchangeable.
- Develop interests in new areas to face fresh challenges.
- Value time off e.g. pursue physical activity, have a baby.
- Maintain social life.
- Avoid self-medication.

Professional
- Choose the right post for you.
- Part-time GPs have a lower rate of burnout.
- Consider extra role e.g. a special interest.
- Have a mentor from another practice.
- Take some study leave (everyone does it!).
- Delegate (try it – it feels good).
- Aim for realistic consultation rate.
- Time management e.g. regular breaks, prioritize, plan ahead.

- Flexibility of work-patterns.
- Government initiatives alter workload in different ways e.g. increase recruitment.
- Work towards fair and supportive practice environment.
- Air all concerns at regular meetings.
- Be assertive and fight for fair and balanced decision-making in the practice.

If needing further help
- Seek confidential third party help e.g. colleagues if appropriate.
- Stress management programmes.
- Own GP to allow yourself the best available care.
- Advice from LMC adviser, mentor or National Counselling Service for sick doctors.

RELEVANT LITERATURE

Avoiding burnout in general practice. Chambers, R *BJGP* **43:** 442–443, 1993.
Avoidable pressures could relieve doctor's stress. Dillner, L *BMJ* **304:** 1587, 1992.

29. Mrs Mowner comes to see you with a request to refer her to a herbalist or a reflexologist as she thinks it may help her asthma. What do you think of this situation and the issues it brings up?

INTRODUCTION

Complementary medicine is popular and used by up to 30% of the population. It represents a large and heterogeneous array of techniques.

FIVE POINT PLAN

Reasons for such requests
- Need to explore her expectations of complementary therapies.
- Why does she think this will work?
- Provision of a pleasant, non-invasive experience of "high touch, low tech" therapy.
- Perceived effectiveness regardless of evidence.
- Perceived safety – "it's natural" (but so are snakebites!).
- Gives optimism and a greater sense of self-control.
- Reports suggest high satisfaction with time spent.
- Patients favour the holistic approach and in-depth explanations.
- More likely to use if dissatisfied with conventional care and last consultation.

Doctors self-awareness
- May feel annoyed or threatened.
- Does this request represent a failure of communication or treatment?
- Opinion depends on personal knowledge and prejudices.
- Take care not to appear to endorse unproven therapies.

Consultation issues
- What is her asthma control and psychological status really like?
- Whatever your stance you need to sort out her asthma first!
- How can you advise on a safe practitioner in an unregulated subject?
- Is there a facility you would be prepared to recommend?
- Creates fragmented uncoordinated care.
- Ensure she has list of her medications to discuss interactions with her new caregiver.

Risk-benefit equation
- Inconsistent standards of training and regulation of alternative practitioners.
- Dearth of high quality trials of effectiveness and safety.
- Many herbal medicines have been doctored with clinically used medicines e.g. steroids.
- Concern that they may contain toxic or carcinogenic ingredients.

- May risk missed or delayed diagnosis.
- Patients may stop or refuse effective conventional treatment.
- Patients may waste money on ineffective treatments.
- Being ineffective does not mean they are not doing any good!

Wider issues
- Who pays? Who should pay?
- 40% of UK GP practices offer access to complementary services such as chiropractic, osteopathy and acupuncture.
- Herbal remedies avoid regulation by being food supplements in the UK.
- Regulation is developing – General Osteopathic Council and a General Chiropractic Council have now been established.
- Therapies have a responsibility to show effectiveness.
- Should we integrate with alternative practitioners and facilitate research?
- Is this a warning to doctors that we are not sufficiently patient-centred?
- Courses on herbalism are now offered at universities which should offer environment of critical analysis and debate.
- Medical school curricula now involve these approaches.

RELEVANT LITERATURE

The role of complementary and alternative medicine. Ernst, E *BMJ* **321:** 1133–1135, 2000.
Complementary medicine. Vickers, A *BMJ* **321:** 683–686, 2000.
Complementary medicine and the doctor. Zollman, C *et al., BMJ* **319:** 1558, 1999.
What can general practice learn from complementary medicine? White, P *BJGP* **50(10):** 821–823, 2000.

INTRODUCTION

Violence is a behaviour which causes anxiety, fear and disruption in practice staff. Over 90% of GPs can expect to be verbally abused, 18% attacked and 11% injured in the line of duty. More than 97% of incidents can be resolved with good communication skills.

Reports suggest the problem is increasing. The Zero Tolerance Zone Campaign seems to have been successful so far in increasing the profile of violence against NHS staff.

FIVE POINT PLAN

Prevention
- Avoid prolonged waiting times.
- Ensure staff are courteous and helpful.
- Wariness of strangers e.g. new temporary resident.
- Avoid dangerous times e.g. one staff member locking up alone.
- Inform others where you are going.
- Be aware of exits.
- Take extra care on night visits.

Recognition
- Best predictor is a history of violent behaviour.
- Other predictors are severe stress, loss of social support, housing etc.
- Index of suspicion for use of drugs and alcohol.
- Observe body language: glaring eyes, loud voice, pacing, argumentative behaviour, repetitive movements, swearing, hands above the waist.

Practice initiatives
- Clear policy that violence will not be tolerated.
- Staff training to recognise warning signs.
- Share information on dangerous patients. Identify and tag notes.
- Prepare guidelines for contingency planning (zero tolerance stand).
- Local health authority may have guidance documents.
- Panic alarm drills.
- Set up reporting system for untoward incidents.
- Attend violence awareness courses.

Premises
- Calm, comfortable waiting area easily observed by receptionists.
- Reduce potential weapons in the consulting room.
- Ensure quick getaway.
- Designated parking near the surgery.
- Police will advise on security issues.

Defusing the situation

- Keep calm and try not to appear intimidated.
- Be open but avoid direct confrontation.
- Active listening with good non-threatening eye contact.
- Lower your voice to the extent to which the patient raises his.
- If in danger, leave the room.
- If in danger, use personal alarms/panic button/call the police.
- Legal entitlement to use reasonable force as last resort if you feel proficient.
- Always debrief and support staff afterwards allowing opportunity for discussion.
- Follow up the patient and explore the reasons for the incident. Some practices draw up a contract of acceptable behaviour.

RELEVANT LITERATURE

Managing violence in general practice. Vickers, K *Update* 241–249, March 2003.

31. Mark is 13 years old and attends the asthma clinic for review without his mother. During the session he admits to using cannabis regularly. What issues does this raise?

INTRODUCTION

This is a difficult situation but it is also an opportunity while seeing Mark alone to tackle some of the issues he is pointing out.

FIVE POINT PLAN

Patient-related issues
- Why is a minor attending alone – was it to bring this subject up?
- Why today? Are there hidden issues?
- What is his level of parental supervision and relationship with his parents?
- Awareness of risks and ability to understand the pros and cons.
- Does he want help to stop the cannabis?
- Level of peer pressure.
- Independent enough to attend surgery on his own but is he mature enough to make a sensible decision?

Doctor issues
- Doctor–patient relationship must be good for patient to confide in you.
- Knowledge of the family.
- Awareness of discomfort and uncertainty of exactly what to do.
- Personal feelings on use of cannabis.

Consultation issues
- Medical asthma review – use of medication, inhaler technique, and control of symptoms.
- Open non-threatening chat about his admission.
- If he also smokes tobacco, need to advise against this.
- Assess his knowledge and provide information on cannabis to fill the gaps.
- Cannabis use may affect schooling and performance at sport.
- Advise that his fitness and sport may improve if he stops.
- Offer written information and plan to see again.

Ethical/legal aspects
- Patient autonomy.
- Confidentiality – assure patient of confidentiality. Would he allow you to talk to parents?
- Legality – will you remind him he is breaking the law?
- Is he in any trouble with the law otherwise?
- Can discuss with defence union if in doubt about responsibilities.

Drug misuse
- Cannabis argument – legalization, prohibition or non-prosecution?
- Slows reaction time, twice as carcinogenic as tobacco, precipitates psychosis in the vulnerable, high levels of dependence.
- Is it a gateway drug?
- But medical potential for research into refined cannabinoids.
- High costs of policing versus social costs of legalization.
- Need for drug misuse educational programmes in schools.
- Media making drugs and smoking glamorous.

RELEVANT LITERATURE

Improving the quality of the cannabis debate: defining the different domains. Strang, J *et al.*, *BMJ* **320:**108–110, 2000.

INTRODUCTION

Chlamydia has been recognized by the Chief Medical Officer's Expert Advisory Group as a condition which requires detailed preventative strategy.

ANSWER PLAN

Requirements of screening

These are described by Wilson's criteria (modified to the acronym "IATRO-GENIC")

- **I**mportant condition.
  Chlamydia causes significant morbidity and associated costs.
- **A**cceptable treatment for the disease.
  It is cheap, effective and safe but more research is needed for acceptability and cost-effectiveness.
- **T**reatment (and diagnostic) facilities available.
  Various setting are available e.g. GUM clinic, GP.
- **R**ecognizable latent or early symptomatic stage.
  A variety of techniques identify asymptomatic stage.
- **O**pinions on who to treat are agreed.
  Local arrangements for partner notification to be agreed.
- **G**uaranteed safety and reliability of test.
  DNA amplification tests have increased the feasibility.
- **E**xamination acceptable to patient.
  Yes in GUM clinics but needs further assessment in GP. Urine test should be acceptable.
- **N**atural history of disease is known.
  Very considerable advances have been made.
- **I**nexpensive and simple test.
  Simple and cheap, cost-effectiveness to be assessed
- **C**ontinuous rolling programme not just a one-off.
  Work needed on the problem of reinfection and contact tracing.

Important issues with chlamydia screening

- The most common curable sexually transmitted infection in the UK with a prevalence of 3–4%.
- Complications are very difficult to treat e.g. pelvic inflammatory disease (PID), tubal infertility and ectopic pregnancy.
- Latent stage is asymptomatic in 70% of women but recognizable with testing.
- Screening programmes exist in the US and Sweden. Screening in

America has led to a 56% reduction in the incidence of PID.

- Testing has become more acceptable with the development of tests based on nucleic acid amplification such as the ligase chain reaction (LCR) which can be performed on urine samples avoiding the need for endocervical swabs.
- Multiple modalities of testing are appropriate e.g. if a smear is being performed anyway.
- Cost-effectiveness in primary care has yet to be clearly established but seems likely to be favourable.
- Guidelines on who to screen have been suggested – all symptomatic women, those seeking terminations, women under 25 opportunistically and those over 25 with a recent change in partner. The latter has been shown to improve detection.
- Important specific barriers are the logistics of contact tracing and psychosocial consequences.
- Evidence shows women respond to a positive test result for the chlamydia infection with shock, unhappiness, embarrassment and worry. Contact tracing causes further embarrassment. There are perceptions of stigma, uncertainty about reproductive health after diagnosis and anxieties regarding partner's reaction to diagnosis.
- Early pilots show that one in ten girls screened tested positive but prevalence will be reduced only if screening is widely offered in general practice.
- A comprehensive approach to a solid infrastructure will be needed before a large initiative. Information provided should normalize and destigmatize chlamydial infection. Support services should be available because notification of partner can cause anxiety. Anxiety about future reproductive morbidity given the uncertain natural history of chlamydia, may prove difficult to dispel.

RELEVANT LITERATURE

Principles and practice of screening for disease. Wilson, J M J and Junger, G *WHO Public Health Paper*, Geneva,1968.
Screening for genital chlamydial infection: the agenda for general practice. (Editorial) Stokes, T *et al.*, *BJGP* **49:** 427–428,1999.
Screening for chlamydia trachomatis. Boag, F *BMJ* **316:** 1474,1998.
Qualitative analysis of psychosocial impact of diagnosis of Chlamydia trachomatis: implications for screening. Duncan, B *et al.*, *BMJ* **322:** 195–199, 2001.
Summary and Conclusions of CMO's Expert Advisory Group on Chlamydia trachomatis. *Dept of Health*, www.doh.gov.uk.

33. A 65 year old retired railway worker with secondaries from his inoperable rectal carcinoma is under your care. He has conveyed his feelings that he is aware he is dying and wishes to do so peacefully at home and not to suffer unnecessarily. He is on the highest dose of morphine that you have encountered and is still bed-bound and in pain. You call to visit. What is your approach?

INTRODUCTION

Care of the terminally ill affects all GPs. It involves careful consultation skills, effective teamwork and knowledge of palliative care with continual reassessment as agreed with the patient and his attendees.

FIVE POINT PLAN

The doctor–patient relationship
- The need to respond to patient's personal desires and needs.
- Patient may fear loss of dignity and self control.
- Assess quality of life.
- Assess psychological status e.g. signs of depression.
- Be open and supportive but clear that you cannot hasten death.
- Ongoing reassurance of relief from pain.

Treatment issues
- Symptom control is clearly inadequate and will need review.
- May require NSAID or opiate syringe driver.
- Need for anxiolytic or antidepressant?
- Attention to constipation, mouth care, pressure points etc.

Family issues
- Be sensitive to the input from spouse and family.
- Answer any questions and respond to their concerns.
- Awareness that duty of confidentiality to patient still exists.

Primary care teamwork
- Encourage input from all members of the multidisciplinary team.
- Named co-ordinator of care is usually the GP.
- The district nurse will be of particular importance.
- Plan for contingencies.
- Good communication regarding your plans on visiting.
- Need for coordination with specialist palliative care.
- Need for ongoing training in palliative care.
- Back-up from Macmillan nurses or Marie Curie nurses.

Legal/ethical issues
- Awareness that doctors are not able to end life at patients' request.
- Discuss role of advance directives.

- Euthanasia is illegal in the UK at present although in some countries is not prosecuted if performed according to protocol.
- Consider personal ethics if asked for advice on how to take life.
- The doctrine of double effect.

RELEVANT LITERATURE

ABC of Palliative Care: Communication with patients, families and other professionals. Faulkner, A *BMJ* **316:** 130–132, 1998.

INTRODUCTION

Strong evidence supports the need for tight glycaemic control and intensive blood pressure management in diabetics. This is best provided by a well-structured framework in primary care.

FIVE POINT PLAN

Define objectives
- Select baseline and follow-up parameters.
- Target risk factors.
- Decide priorities e.g. tight glucose control, strict BP control, statin therapy, use of aspirin.
- Evidence has shown that intensive glycaemic control improves risk for many diabetic complications in Type 1 and 2 diabetes especially microvascular pathology.

Define methods
- Opportunistic or clinic-based? i.e. normal surgery time, mini-clinics or "diabetic days".
- Consider length of appointment times.
- Discuss methods of case-finding e.g. computerized prescriptions.
- Effective registers and recall system.
- Criteria for intervention e.g. use of risk tables.
- Meetings with relevant parties e.g. local diabetologist and community diabetic nurse.
- Evidence has shown that lack of structure of diabetic care is associated with increased mortality but organisational improvements can achieve equivalent standards or better.

Primary care team issues
- The need for a motivated team.
- Nominated doctor and nurse as well as chiropodist/optometrist.
- Agree practice treatment protocols based on accepted evidence or guidelines.
- Consider skill mix and assess need for training.
- Use of the shared care model.

Management issues
- Resources and financing e.g. need for special equipment.
- Practicalities of keeping register of diabetic patients e.g. note-tagging.
- Inclusion in practice brochure.

Review and audit

- Failsafes e.g. review of defaulters.
- Regular assessment of performance criteria e.g. percentage of patients with tight glycaemic control/BP control, percentage receiving regular review, patients with updated management plans.
- Feedback from patients.

RELEVANT LITERATURE

UKPDS. The UK Prospective Diabetic Study. *BMJ* **317:** 703–720, 1998.
Diabetes care in general practice: meta-analysis of randomised controlled trials.
 Griffin, S *BMJ* **317:** 390–396, 1998.
The National Service Framework for Diabetes. *Dept of Health.*

35. Evaluate the impact of NHS walk-in centres in the following areas.
  • Use by patients.
  • Cost-benefit issues.
  • Appropriateness of service.
  • The future.

INTRODUCTION

Walk-in centres were announced in 1999 as a response to demand and changing needs as a new and separately funded government-backed initiative.

ANSWER PLAN

Use by patients
- Has been a gradual but steady increase in the number of visitors.
- Increased use by young and middle-aged men who have previously underused services.
- Reasons included speed and convenience of access as well as anonymity.
- Attracts more affluent group (owner-occupiers) increasing inequalities to accessing health care.
- Has not increased use of services by disadvantaged groups/minorities.
- More likely to attend on day one of illness.
- Few patients took advantage of attending in the evening.
- More attended if already located on hospital sites.

Cost-benefit issues
- Evidence of high patient satisfaction.
- Less popularity with elderly, less affluent and less mobile.
- Quality of nurse care high for a limited range of problems. Figures only relate to nurse practitioners with extended training.
- Provide safe care of high quality – 85% of consultations are from nurses with a median consultation time of 14 minutes.
- Difficult to compare true quality to GP due to different case mix e.g. minor injury vs. chronic disease management.
- Cost estimated as nearly 50% higher than a GP consultation.
- Costs to the NHS appear expensive.

Appropriateness of service
- One in six had previous contact with doctor or nurse for the same illness episode.
- Low referral rates might imply service is appropriate as only 13% were referred to their GP. A third went anyway.
- Lack of continuity of care is not an issue for providers or patients in this setting.

- Failure of aims to target disadvantaged.
- Patients tended to lack knowledge that they would be treated by a nurse without full prescribing powers.
- Wide variation in structure e.g. minor injury units in hospital or shopping centre facilities.
- Lack of evidence of significant reduction in demand on GPs, A&E or out-of hours services.
- GP workload still rose even if a walk-in centre was nearby.

The future
- Resources may be better used for those with higher health needs.
- Centres generally successful but need to compare alternatives which may be a better way to target needier patients.
- An obvious model is to give GPs funds to employ nurses to treat patients in a designated walk-in practice in each town. This will also help achieve 48 hour access targets.
- Although most GPs thought walk-in centres undermined continuity, they may be won over by being more closely involved.

RELEVANT LITERATURE

What is the role of walk-in centres in the NHS? Salisbury, C *et al.*, *BMJ* **324:** 399–402, 2002.
The National Evaluation of NHS Walk-in Centres: Final Report. *University of Bristol,* July 2002, www.epi.bris.ac.uk/wic/publications.htm.

INTRODUCTION

Suicide attempts often present to Accident and Emergency but this case may be more sensitively handled initially by the GP.

FIVE POINT PLAN

Patient's problems
- What effect did she feel the tablets would have?
- Explore feelings, motivations and circumstances leading up to it.
- Possible reasons of escape, attention-seeking or manipulation.
- May have deeper issues e.g. physical or sexual abuse.
- Presence or absence of a supportive social network.
- Use of alcohol or substance misuse.

Doctor's agenda
- Sensitive consultation skills to achieve rapport.
- See patient alone and together with parents.
- Ask about any sexual history.
- Awareness that the overdose will do little harm.
- Concern over the leaving of a note.
- Is there sign of a major depression or genuine suicidal intent?
- Evaluate short-term risk of suicide as your experience allows.
- Assess family's ability to cope.

Family issues
- Discuss recent behaviour and course of events.
- Discuss changes in family dynamics and home circumstances.
- Would she have known that the parents would be home soon?
- How are parents reacting?

Legal/confidentiality issues
- Ensure confidentiality as best you can.
- Below age of heterosexual consent (if relevant).
- Under 16 year olds with sufficient intelligence and understanding can consent to medical treatment but refusal to consent is not legally binding if the parents give consent in the child's best interests.

Management
- Discussion with Poisons Unit if unsure of toxicity.
- Is there depression sufficient to need acute admission (rare)?
- Discuss strategies with all present.

- Express concern (10% will commit suicide within 10 years).
- Offer practical solutions to practical problems if possible.
- Gain agreement with all about the way forward.
- Arrange early review appointment.
- Consider later secondary referral if needed.

RELEVANT LITERATURE

Managing self-harm: the legal issues. *DTB* **35(6):** 43–46, 1997.
Management of deliberate self-harm in general practice: a qualitative study. Prasad, L R *et al.*, *BJGP* **49:** 721–724, 1999.
Management of patients who deliberately harm themselves. Isacsson, G *BMJ* **322:** 213–215, 2001.

INTRODUCTION

NICE has criticized organizational problems in primary care with regards to epileptics. It has noted a lack of management plans and poor record-keeping.

ANSWER PLAN

Possible models

Some form of jointly managed shared-care between GPs and hospital consultants with enhanced exchange of information is widely seen as the preferred model.

Examples include the following.

- Community clinics where a specialist, perhaps a GP with special interest, runs a clinic in the practice.
- Basic model where letters are sent after attendances but also regular updates are sent so exceeding the normal communication.
- Liaison meetings where a case review meeting with all carers is held to decide on joint management plan.
- Co-operation cards carried by patient between carers and documenting an agreed dataset.
- Computer-assisted care where all information is inputted to hospital computer with updates and advice sent in a standardized way back to GP.
- Electronic mail – common database with multiple entry and access points available to all members of the team.

Example of care plan

Initiating treatment
- Local protocols for epileptics can facilitate diagnosis and referral.
- Telephone/Email contact with specialist can allow initiation of drug therapy.
- Printed information can be supplied.

Continuing care
- Agreed datasets for chronic management can simplify treatment.
- Updated computer records allows at-a-glance assessment of control.
- Clinical nurse specialists can help liaise with medical team.

Information and advice
- Patient-held records can be a personal source of information and encourage problem ownership.

- Patient protocols can advise on accessing help.
- Agree written advice on issues of driving, use of a seizure diary, free prescriptions, personal drug regime, avoidance of triggers, contraception etc.

Involvement of other agencies
- District-based workers can continue education and support.
- Clinical nurse can co-ordinate with schools, employers, family and carers.
- Patient organizations e.g. National Society for Epilepsy, British Epilepsy Association, offer information and support.

Audit
- Teamwork allows combination of practice-based/district-based and hospital-based audit.

RELEVANT LITERATURE

Diagnosis and management of epilepsy in adults – a national clinical guideline. *SIGN Guideline No 21, Nov 1997.*

38. **Discuss errors and their prevention in primary care with regard to the following.**
   - **Prescribing errors.**
   - **Errors in communication and organization.**

INTRODUCTION

General practice provides longitudinal personalized care that is customized to individual beliefs, needs, values, and preferences across a broad spectrum of concerns relating to health and illness. Resultant variations in practice make the assessment of "error" complex.

ANSWER PLAN

Prescribing

- Prescribing problems affect 3–5% of all prescriptions, a third of these can be classified as major safety concerns.
- Large number of complaints relate to prescription of contraindicated drugs e.g. due to errors in dispensing, ignoring known allergies.
- The most easily analyzed area of medical review but increasingly complex as polypharmacy increases.
- Seriousness ranges from minor to terminal.
- Principles of underuse (e.g. not prescribing an ACE inhibitor in heart failure).
- Principles of overuse (of antibiotics everywhere).
- Principle of misuse (wrong drug prescribed).
- Interactions of unknown herbal medications taken by the patient.
- Errors may include decision-making skills or issues of knowledge.
- Secondary contributing causes may include budgeting concerns.
- Identification of errors may come from yourself, colleagues, pharmacists, receptionist, nurses, relatives or patients.
- Evidence suggests a computer system can aid safe prescribing but may also create new errors e.g. lack of human review of repeat prescriptions.
- Community pharmacist assistance can have a major impact here.
- Audits should take place in such areas enabling error to be actively sought out.

Communication and organization

- Examples of breakdown of communication/organization include lack of formality of information transfer to colleagues, failing to monitor INR in a warfarin user, failing to follow up a smear result.
- Fewer layers of bureaucracy and an already strong structure of teamwork to build on in primary care may make solutions easier than in hospitals.
- Patient-held records can allow shared access for different health workers.

- Need for mechanism to prioritize important messages e.g. use of message book in the practice which is checked and signed by all.
- Electronic types of communication and record-keeping can improve success.
- Many safety problems can be overcome by identifying the systems of errors and adjusting their design.
- Use of clinical governance and significant event analysis will help prevent further errors.
- A new safety culture of openness is required with a no-blame approach to allow identification of the system failures.

RELEVANT LITERATURE

Organisation with a memory. *Dept. of Health*, 2000.
Building a safer NHS. *Dept. of Health*, 2001.
Enhancing public safety in primary care. Wilson, T *et al.*, *BMJ* **324:** 584–587, 2002.

39. Mr. Rutter is 55 years and has come to see you after his third blood pressure measurement. The readings have averaged at 165/105. He is adamant that he is not prepared to take medication. How do you proceed?

INTRODUCTION

Hypertension is an important risk factor for MI and vascular disease but lack of compliance with medication is a widespread problem.

FIVE POINT PLAN

Patient's agenda
- Explore ideas and concerns, reasons for non-compliance.
- Is there denial of illness?
- May be unaware of importance.
- Are there reversible stresses e.g. occupational?

Doctor's agenda
- Is this a sign of a poor doctor–patient relationship?
- Take appropriate history.
- Assess risk factors (smoking, family history, exercise, diabetes etc.).
- Examination for end-organ damage e.g. fundoscopy, carotid bruit, peripheral pulses.
- Investigation e.g. urinalysis, U&E, blood sugar, cholesterol.
- Issues of keeping up to date with latest recommendations.

Sharing information
- Forge good relationship to build on in the future.
- Explanation of pros and cons of treatment.
- Explanation of possible side effects of medication.
- Lifestyle advice/non-drug treatment.
- Direct efforts to overcome possible non-compliance.

Practice organization
- Need to tag patient to monitor BP in future
- Use of risk-assessment tables and nurse review clinics

Management plan
- Achieve common understanding.
- Agree on treatment plan.
- If accepts medication, use evidence-based guidelines.
- Respect his decision rather than waste a prescription.
- If no agreement on medication, make substitute plan to monitor and review while emphasizing lifestyle changes.
- Arrange follow-up regardless – planned or opportunistic.
- Keep good record of discussion and decisions.

RELEVANT LITERATURE

British Hypertension Society guidelines for hypertension management: summary.
  BMJ **319:** 630–635,1999.

INTRODUCTION

Various formularies have existed for some time e.g. BNF, MIMS. Specific general practice formularies have also been published.

A preferred list of medications that are agreed for use in the surgery may benefit a practice. GPs are responsible for 75% of NHS prescribing.

ANSWER PLAN

Advantages
- Consistency (medication agreed by partners).
- Use as an educational tool.
- Helps prevent drug-induced illness.
- Cuts prescribing costs.
- Encourages generic prescribing.
- Promotes contact with hospital consultants and pharmacists.
- Opportunity to audit prescribing.
- Reduces external influences e.g. drug companies.
- Aid for registrars/locums.
- May be able to access via computer.
- Aid for limited nurse prescribing e.g. dressings.
- Can put level 3 PACT data into practice.

Disadvantages
- Rigidity – prevents adoption of new ideas.
- Limits autonomy and application of personal experience.
- Not always beneficial cost-wise.
- Hospitals may initiate non-formulary drugs.
- Time-consuming exercise.
- Resistance of doctors to change.
- Reluctance of patients to change to formulary drugs e.g. generics.
- Difficulty reaching practice agreement.
- Requirement for updating regularly.

RELEVANT LITERATURE

Constructing a practice formulary: a learning exercise. *DTB* **29(7)** July 1991.

41. You are visited by a 30 year old mother and her 4 year old son who has previously been diagnosed by a specialist with a hyperactive disorder. She complains that she has just been asked to remove him from nursery due to his disruptive behaviour. She appears at the end of her tether. How do you approach the problem?

INTRODUCTION

Up to 5% of children can be classified as having Attention Deficit Hyperactivity Disorder (ADHD). It affects males three times more frequently than females and the core features are inattention, overactivity and impulsiveness.

FIVE POINT PLAN

Patient and family issues
- Assess mother's expectations.
- Evaluate her knowledge of the diagnosis.
- Assess her ability to cope, psychological status and other underlying problems.
- Environmental factors e.g. adequate housing, and level of disruption at home.
- Suitable support network and family dynamics?

Doctor and consultation issues
- Background knowledge of the family to provide context.
- Will be a challenging and time-consuming consult. Are you up to date?
- The need for good communication skills to assess where the problems lie.
- Empathetic style to help ease her demoralization.
- Observe mother–child interaction.
- Need to be positive and supportive for the family.
- Offer simple advice to avoid triggers and encourage routine.
- May need to terminate a lengthy consultation and arrange follow-up.

Diagnostic issues
- No test can confirm the diagnosis of ADHD.
- Check notes – was ADHD actually diagnosed?
- Is a specialist paediatrician still involved in the case?
- Was medication prescribed and still taken?
- GP will have a role in monitoring therapy if prescribed.

Multidisciplinary team
- Attempt to get input from everyone involved in the case e.g. nursery teacher for underlying story.
- Important to keep child in normal societal settings if at all possible.
- Additional input from health visitor.

- Need for referral back to specialist for diagnosis and behavioural therapy?

Wider issues
- Are there support groups available locally?
- Concerns of worldwide overuse of stimulants in ADHD but possible underdiagnosis in UK.
- NICE guidance confirms drugs are to be prescribed by specialists but may be monitored by GPs with shared care.
- Many parents seek unproven alternative therapies.

RELEVANT LITERATURE

The management of hyperactive children. *DTB* **33(8)**: 37, 1995.
Attention deficit hyperactivity disorder – a review. Williams, C *et al.*, *BJGP* **49**: 563–71,1999.
Attention-deficit hyperactivity disorder. Thapar, A *et al.*, *BJGP* **53**: 225–230, 2003.

INTRODUCTION

Around 30 000 drug misusers are identified on the Regional Drug Misuse Databases. The balance is towards males in the ratio 3:1 and over half report heroin as their major drug of misuse. The average GP may see one to two new cases per year. In recent years there has been a marked increase in drug-related deaths in the 15–19 year age group. Harm minimization is seen by the Dept of Health as a valuable and attainable goal and the next best thing to abstinence.

FIVE POINT PLAN

Patient-related issues
- Why is she presenting now?
- Consider the possibility of underlying reasons for presenting.
- Explore patient's beliefs regarding own health and effects of drugs.
- Is she motivated to change?
- What are her expectations of you?
- Social circumstances and home support.
- Ongoing problems with the law.

Issues for the doctor
- Initial management of the presenting complaint.
- Use non-judgemental consultation technique to gain mutual trust and start to approach the problem.
- Awareness of personal prejudices.
- Concerns over personal ability, experience and need for training in dealing with drug misuse e.g. awareness of range of local services.
- Minimum requirement is provision of care for all general health needs and drug-related problems.
- Adequate history of drug problem and proper management of the presenting complaint.
- General health assessment including psychiatric morbidity.
- Generally supportive approach and further advice in specific areas.

Issues for the practice
- All doctors need to be able to treat drug misusers.
- Responsibility to provide care.
- Development of agreed practice policy/use of guidelines.
- Concerns over increased workload with demanding patient group.
- Consider designating time, resources, named doctor.
- Possibility of extra funding from the health authority.
- Concerns over safety and harassment of staff.

Treatment issues
- Advice on risk reduction behaviour to limit harm.
- Supportive role.
- Avoidance of prescribing substitute medication in isolation.
- Comprehensive record-keeping.
- Follow-up plan.
- Agreement with pharmacists for supervision of substitute medication.
- Shared-care model utilises different skills most effectively.
- Principle of harm limitation i.e. use of sterile equipment, needle-exchange programmes, discuss blood-borne viral infection, HIV testing, offer hepatitis B vaccination, sexual precautions.
- Patient's need to be conscious about own health needs.
- Invitation to contact specialist services e.g. community drug teams.

Legal/ethical issues
- Notification to the Home Office Addicts Index is advisable but no longer compulsory.
- High rate of criminal behaviour amongst users.
- Special licence from Home Office required for diamorphine prescription.

RELEVANT LITERATURE

Drug Misuse and Dependence – Guidelines on Clinical Management. *Dept. of Health 1999.*
Helping patients who misuse drugs. *DTB* **35(3):** 23–24, 1997.
The management of opioid dependence. *MeReC Bulletin* **12(4):** 13–16, March 2002.

Evaluate the evidence for the following in the diagnosis and treatment of heart failure.
- **Beta-blockers.**
- **Aldosterone antagonists.**
- **Brain natriuretic peptide.**
- **Angiotensin II receptor antagonists.**

ANSWER PLAN

Beta-blockers
- Used to be contraindicated.
- Research in mild to moderate heart failure has shown a 37% relative risk reduction for death and hospitalization in favour of beta-blockers.
- Evaluation in nearly 10 000 patients with chronic heart failure in over 20 RCTs shown to decrease the risk of death, hospital admission and to improve patients' clinical status. NNT for first year = 26.
- Evidence that they improve exercise capacity or are as effective in severe heart failure is less robust.
- Research applies to stable patients already on an ACE inhibitor.
- Effects seem to be additive to those of ACE inhibitors.
- Cautious slow titration of the dose – preferably initiated by a specialist.

Aldosterone antagonists
- RALES – the Randomized Aldactone Evaluation Study has shown advantage of adding spironolactone to ACE inhibitors and loop diuretic in moderate to severe heart failure by reducing mortality by 30%.
- Previously contraindicated due to unfounded fear of hyperkalaemia.
- Benefit was mainly due to a 10% absolute risk reduction in death from cardiac causes.
- Gynecomastia/breast pain were common in men.
- Value in less severe disease unclear.

Brain natriuretic peptide
- N-terminal pro-brain natriuretic peptide assay has potential as part of a diagnostic triage in patients presenting with symptoms suggestive of heart failure or in screening high-risk populations.
- May have role as an initial test in a community-screening programme.
- Normal concentrations of NT-proBNP could rule out heart failure in suspected patients due to high negative predictive values.
- Not a good test to "rule in" the diagnosis.
- Normal concentrations virtually exclude the diagnosis of heart failure.
- Very high levels effectively diagnose the condition.
- Intermediate values require confirmation by echocardiography.
- May be cost-effective at £15 per test.

Angiotensin II receptor antagonists

- Angiotensin II receptor blockers are a recent development.
- The ValHeFT trial compared valsartan to placebo and showed 13% improvement in all-cause mortality and morbidity.
- ELITE II showed losartan had similar benefits to captopril but was better tolerated.
- Currently there is no persuasive evidence they are superior to ACE inhibitors in treating heart failure but have a role when ACE inhibitors are poorly tolerated or contraindicated.

RELEVANT LITERATURE

The diagnosis and drug treatment of heart failure. *MeReC Briefing No 15* Aug 2001.

Drug treatment in heart failure. Lonn, E *et al., BMJ* **320:** 1188–1192, 2000.

Reliability of N-terminal pro-brain natriuretic peptide assay in diagnosis of heart failure: cohort study in representative and high-risk community populations. Hobbs, F D R *et al., BMJ* **324:** 1498, 2002.

INTRODUCTION

The population is becoming older and the implications for workload can be considerable.

FIVE POINT PLAN

Implications for the partners
- Need to arrange meeting to make considered decision.
- Policies on visits/prescribing/admission to hospital.
- Increased workload in a high morbidity group.
- Any additional income for non-NHS services?
- Would areas of special interest or expertise amongst partners be of value?
- Availability of specialist community nurses to help improve care.

Practice issues
- Rearrangement of duties.
- Shared workload or nominated doctor?
- Is there an ongoing requirement or desire for preventative health checks?
- Development of protocols e.g. detection of diabetics.
- Organization of prescriptions.

Issues for patients
- Loss of autonomy as may prefer to keep own GP.
- Loss of continuity of care.

Decision
- Is the home sufficiently well organized and motivated to facilitate your plans to modernize care?
- You may be the only practice in the area in which case there may be no choice.
- Otherwise need to avoid offending other practices in the neighbourhood.

Future plans
- Evidence suggests there is lack of organized medical input and sub-optimal care in nursing homes with underdiagnosis of problems that can be eased.
- Homes paying local GPs were more likely to receive one or more additional services, over and above the core contractual obligations. Few homes had direct access to specialists.

- These variations raise serious questions about patient autonomy and equitable levels of care for all.
- GP care of nursing home residents will be optional under the new contract.
- NSF Framework for Older People aims to give them access to a new range of enhanced intermediate care services to promote independence.

RELEVANT LITERATURE

Managing diabetes in residential and nursing homes. Tattersall, R *et al., BMJ* **316:** 89, 1998.

A survey of access to medical services in nursing and residential homes in England. Glendinning, C *et al., BJGP* **52(7):** 545–548, 2002.

National Service Framework for Older People. *Dept. of Health,* March 2001.

45. "Lifestyle interventions are important in the secondary prevention of coronary heart disease". What is the evidence for this?

INTRODUCTION

Coronary heart disease is the single largest cause of death in the UK.

Direct costs to the health service and social security were £1.6 billion in 1996. Indirect costs to the economy reach £10 billion each year.

There is now clear evidence of the benefit of promoting lifestyle changes in patients who have already suffered MI.

ANSWER PLAN

Smoking cessation
- Reduces chance of further non-fatal MI and cardiovascular mortality by 50%.
- Brief advice from the GP can achieve 5% cessation.
- Reduces risk of post-infarction angina.
- Observational studies suggest CHD risk falls rapidly to the level of a non-smoker by 3 years.
- Stroke risk can remain elevated for 5–10 years and all-cause mortality for 15 years.
- Advice, counselling therapies, nicotine replacement therapy and bupropion are all effective.

Diet
- The DART trial (Diet and Reinfarction Trial) took oily fish or fish oil supplements (which are high in omega 3 fatty acids) and reduced total mortality by 29% over 2 years. Two portions a week are advised.
- No significant reduction in cardiac events overall due to counterbalancing by increase in non-fatal MI. May have anti-arrythmic effect in sudden death?
- Difference at 10 years was less marked perhaps due to fewer differences in oily fish consumption.
- Cochrane review of 27 RCTs for reduced or modified dietary fat showed a small but important reduction in cardiovascular risk in trials over 2 years.
- Cardioprotective or Mediterranean diet high in nuts, fruit and vegetables is better than a standard low-fat diet in reducing coronary risk.
- Advice for five portions of fruit and vegetables per day has been shown to reduce cardiac events post-MI and brief nurse intervention is successful at increasing compliance.
- Lack of evidence for salt restriction on cardiac morbidity but probably reduces BP.
- Evidence for vitamin supplements/garlic is unconvincing.
- Lack of hard evidence for plant sterols and stanols e.g. in Benecol.

- Inverse association between BMI and long term risk of reinfarction.

Alcohol
- Moderate consumption of alcohol has protective effect reducing CHD by 30–35%.
- Two to three glasses of wine per day are considered beneficial.
- Meta-analysis of good quality studies found 1 to 2 units per day gave a RR reduction of 20% for CHD but showed a risk increase at around 7 units per day.
- Lack of consensus about optimal type of beverage.
- Advice is "moderation".

Exercise
- Exercise-based rehabilitation (Cochrane review) may reduce cardiac death but research is of a poor quality.
- Positive effects on weight, BP, diabetes, osteoporosis.
- Best combined with a lifestyle intervention programme.
- Absolute risk of further MI after exercise is small and benefits outweigh risks.

Rehabilitation programmes
- Cardiac rehabilitation can reduce cardiovascular mortality from heart failure and further MI by 25%.
- Nurse-led clinics in primary care facilitate optimal secondary prevention.
- Stress reduction is part of most rehabilitation programmes but few firm data are available.

RELEVANT LITERATURE

Lifestyle measures to reduce cardiovascular risk. *MeReC Briefing No 19* Sept. 2002.
Secondary Prevention of Coronary Heart Disease Following Myocardial Infarction. *SIGN Guideline No. 41.*

INTRODUCTION

Medicine in Britain is increasingly a transcultural specialty and it is essential that we try to understand the differences between us that impact on our ability to deliver primary care.

FIVE POINT PLAN

Issues for the patient
- Many ethnic groups believe in demand-led consultation and find appointments inconvenient.
- Often have high expectation of prescription.
- Ethnic minorities often have relatively poor health.
- But research still shows higher consultation rates than would be expected.
- Eastern patients tend to be more frightened of pain and may need more reassurance.
- Erroneous health beliefs e.g. no symptoms means no need for follow up.
- Reluctance over intimate disclosures.
- Illness in a family member can be a crisis for the whole family.

Issues for the doctor
- Early need to clarify patient's agenda.
- Awareness of how personal beliefs influence performance.
- Knowledge of disease prevalence in different groups e.g. persistent cough indicating TB, early onset of diabetes in Asians.
- Respect privacy and dignity with special regard to physical examination.
- Other members of family or advocate may wish to be seen in same appointment slot.

Communication issues
- Language and non-verbal barriers.
- Show respect for a patient's culture, religion and ethnicity by showing awareness, courtesy, understanding and ability to negotiate.
- Avoid transcultural conflict – assure the advocate that Eastern customs will be respected.
- Potential ignorance regarding questions which could cause offence.
- Difficulty in assessing symptoms leading to misdiagnosis.
- How best to offer preventative advice e.g. check on uptake of smear.
- Poor communication may mean poor compliance.
- Need to gradually educate patient.

Role of the advocate/interpreter

- Always accompanies Eastern women and may be relation or friend.
- Might speak for the patient making it a three-way consultation. Family members can become too involved.
- Can act as chaperone, interpreter and mediator.
- Translation includes interpretation and research suggests a high error rate with clinical consequences.
- May report back to the family on your treatment of the patient.

Practice issues

- Consider size of ethnic population and need for interpreting skills.
- Is further training required?
- Implications for workload and consultation times.
- Social measures e.g. housing, still needed to tackle inverse care law.

RELEVANT LITERATURE

Ethnicity in everyday practice. Kelshiker, *Doctor*, Dec. 2002.

47. As the newest partner in the practice, you have inherited Mrs Peabody on you personal list. She has the thickest set of notes in the practice but no serious disease has ever been diagnosed. Your partners seem to find this hilarious and wish you "Good luck". Assuming you stay with this new practice and your new patient, what issues do you consider in her management?

INTRODUCTION

Each GP will have on average 10–15 such patients with chronic medically unexplained physical symptoms (MUPS). The new model for these "somatizers" is of a complex interaction of biological, psychological, social and cultural factors.

FIVE POINT PLAN

Patient-related issues
- Emotional state and social situation may weigh heavily on symptoms.
- May associate symptoms with illness or life events.
- Often have history of illness as a child and poor parental care.
- Interpersonal factors – more relationship difficulties, possibility of abuse.
- Higher likelihood of recurrent depressive disorder.
- High demands and expectations.
- Does patient feel symptoms are genuine or might they deliberately feign symptoms (malingerers)?

Doctor issues
- A wearing time-consuming consultation.
- Awareness of demoralization and anger (yours and hers).
- Who is *your* support and who else can you get involved?
- Do you have the skills for this?
- Awareness of emotional manipulation e.g. "Nobody cares".
- Iatrogenic harm from over-investigation and over-prescribing.

Consultation style
- Keep open the possibility of a physical diagnosis developing i.e. maintain aetiological neutrality (Beware the epitaph of the hypochondriac – "See, I told you I was ill").
- Acknowledge symptoms as real and valid. Avoid false reassurance and retaliation.
- Explore worst fears and react flexibly to her response.
- Provide explanation where possible.
- Employ techniques of "reattribution" to encourage patient to map her symptoms to her psychology rather than her body.
- Check understanding by summarizing back to patient.
- Broaden her agenda each time you see her.

General aspects of management
- Identify one doctor as principal carer.
- Review notes for hidden clues and make summary.
- Plan extended consultation to derive problem list.
- Thorough clinical assessment and appropriate investigation.
- Avoid referral. Unavoidable referrals require specific predefined objectives and liaison with the specialist.
- Withdraw unnecessary drugs and avoid extra ones.
- Repeated examination may reinforce illness behaviour.
- Emphasise learning to cope rather than cure.
- Be proactive about future appointments – discourage appointments outside planned times.
- Is there a relative in whom you could find a therapeutic ally?
- May become a rewarding case in the end.

Evidence-based therapy
- Little data from RCTs.
- A study of 73 patients with MUPS found three patients after 6 years in whom a newly diagnosed organic neurological disorder may have explained their symptoms.
- Helpful measures were explanation of tangible mechanisms behind the symptoms, ascribing symptoms to causes which avoid blame, encouraging self-help strategies.
- Antidepressants can be useful even in the absence of depression.
- Training GPs in reattribution techniques is of value.
- Cognitive behavioural therapy has been shown to help.

RELEVANT LITERATURE

Chronic multiple functional somatic symptoms. Bass, C *et al.*, *BMJ* **325**: 323–326, 2002.

Beyond somatisation: a review of the understanding and treatment of medically unexplained physical symptoms (MUPS). Burton, C *BJGP* **53(3)**: 231–239, 2003.

What to do about medically unexplained symptoms. *DTB* **39(1)**: 5–8, Jan 2001.

INTRODUCTION

Guidelines are defined as systematically developed statements to assist practitioner and patient decisions about appropriate health care for specific clinical circumstances. The National Institute of Clinical Excellence is taking a key role in the production of such guidance.

ANSWER PLAN

Benefits

- Explicitly state practical targets.
- Ensure consistency in the primary care team.
- Can turn knowledge into action by making best and clearest use of data.
- A useful aide-memoire.
- A useful guide for the newcomer to the practice e.g. registrar.
- Can cover all aspects of care e.g. investigation, diagnosis, treatment.
- Evidence has shown in several studies that they can improve delivery of care.
- Likely to be used by those who have helped develop them.
- Can save money.
- Major guidelines could be a reasonable legal defence e.g. those from NICE.

Potential disadvantages

- Require regular updating.
- Require adaptation to the target population.
- Need proper dissemination and promotion to reach GP consciousness.
- May be expensive and impractical to implement.
- Danger of inaccuracy and bias e.g. selective use of evidence.
- Evidence shows passively delivered complex guidelines are ineffective.
- Not a legal standard.
- Guideline overload – there are millions of them!

Construction of guidelines

Decide on objectives

- Identify a clear need.
- Get agreement from those who will use them.
- Decide what needs to be achieved.

Select approach

- Do adaptable guidelines already exist? (try www.eguidelines.co.uk).
- Best available evidence base is the most widely accepted and most valid basis for guidelines.

- Relevant high quality sources are researched, reviewed, critically appraised and summarized.
- Relevant expertise e.g. hospital consultants, librarians, health economists should be consulted as necessary.
- Other less rigorous (and less valid) approaches may take the form of small surveys or consensus opinion.
- One approach may involve central development with regional adaptation to allow "local ownership" of the guidelines.

Writing the guidelines
- The gold standard should incorporate a full account of the risks and benefits of treatment, patient preference and cost-effectiveness.
- Should be clear and appropriate to need.
- Statement of aim and method.
- Statement of who is responsible for each component of care.
- Describe monitoring and recording.
- Describe standards and targets.

Distribution
- Period of discussion, debate and adaptation.
- Disseminate effectively.

Audit and update
- Assess improvement in delivery of patient care.
- Include a date for review as evidence may change.

RELEVANT LITERATURE

Construction and use of guidelines. *Prescriber's Journal,* **39(3):** 1999.
General practitioner's use of guidelines in the consultation and their attitudes to them. Watkins, C *et al., BJGP* **49:** 11–15, 1999.

INTRODUCTION

Prostate cancer is the second commonest cancer in men. Five-year survival is 43% and 30% of men have a latent cancer at death. The UK has no currently accepted screening programme.

FIVE POINT PLAN

Issues for the patient
- Reasons for request and underlying concerns.
- Presence of urinary symptoms – if so assess International Prostate Symptom Score.
- What are his expectations and understanding of the test?
- Issues of patient autonomy i.e. right to choose.

Issues for the doctor
- Government advice is not to routinely screen.
- May be difficult to refuse a direct request.
- Need to be aware of current recommendations.
- Good consultation skills to understand concerns.
- Screen by digital rectal examination? (high sensitivity of abnormality, low specificity).
- Opportunistic advice on cardiac disease might do him more good.

Issues for the practice
- Consider developing practice guidelines on performing prostate-specific antigen (PSA) test.
- Availability of written information.
- How to target men's health issues.
- Availability of practice nurse phlebotomy.

Decision-making
- Need to make a shared decision on whether to go for it.
- Need for informed consent.
- Provide detailed information to enable an informed choice.
- Mr. Albert's motives for going ahead with testing might be the irresistible logic of finding a cancer early, the drive to avoid later regret in not having the test and a perceived right to parity with women's access to screening.
- Doctor and patient will both have to deal with the consequences of agreeing to a test that is not an ideal tool.
- Arrange review for explanation of test result if chosen.

Evidence for screening

- No RCT has shown that routine PSA screening improves lifespan or quality of life.
- But work from the US (where they screen) does suggest a decline in advanced disease in recent years.
- The low positive predictive value of a raised PSA has implied that the test should not be done in the absence of symptoms.
- The most cost-effective approach may be a combination of digital rectal examination and PSA but the high false positive rate is worrying.
- Does not fulfil Wilson's criteria.
- About 10% of men aged 50–69 will have raised PSA, but only about a quarter will be confirmed to have prostate cancer, and some tumours will be missed.
- These high PSAs will all be offered a painful transrectal biopsy.
- One estimate of number needed to test (to save one life) came in at 100. Too high?

RELEVANT LITERATURE

Screening for prostate cancer in the UK. Donovan, J *et al.*, BMJ **323:** 763–764, 2001.

50. **Your practice manager has worked for you for 3 years and done an excellent job. She comes to you requesting partner status and mentions that she has a number of job offers on the "back-burner". What issues are thereby raised?**

INTRODUCTION

A practice needs to be coherent in its response to an unusual request.

FIVE POINT PLAN

Motives
- Why has this request come up now?
- What is her agenda?
- What are her financial aims?
- How does she feel her new status will benefit the practice?
- Does she make a compelling case?

Implications
- How does this alter her role and responsibility?
- What will she actually bring to the group?
- How does this affect the balance of power *re* decision-making?
- Need for legal advice on her and your liabilities.
- What extra competencies would be needed?
- Can you do without her if she does not get her way?

Issues for the partners
- May feel threatened at the phrasing of the request.
- Meet and discuss personal reactions – Good idea? Or "over my dead body"?
- How does the request fit with your knowledge of the individual?
- Do you retain doctors that are not even partners?
- What are the financial implications?
- Are her academic qualifications appropriate?
- Information gathering – are there any precedents? Unforeseen consequences?
- May need discussion with BMA.
- Caution regarding an unusual step for a practice.
- Effect on other staff e.g. receptionists, nurses.

Management of the problem
- Careful explanation of your decision for or against.
- Agreement would retain a happy staff member (or rather fellow partner).
- Formulate initial plan if you agree to her request.
- If not, brush off your best communication skills.
- Reassure that you have given the idea due consideration.
- Is there a compromise position e.g. a pay rise, new title (!)?

Wider issues

- Extended partnerships could include more members of the PHCT e.g. practice nurses.
- New models of primary care are inevitable.

INTRODUCTION

This can be a common request in general practice. How you organize your response is at least as important as what you decide.

FOUR POINT PLAN

Patient-related issues
- Reasons for leaving previous GP e.g. dissatisfaction, geographical.
- Approach has been polite and may deserve a chance.
- Are expectations reasonable?
- Is there a preference for a certain doctor?
- Has he been removed from his previous list?
- Patient autonomy gives the right to shop around.
- Does he live within your catchment area?
- Availability of extended services and modern policies may be different between practices.
- Does the request extend to his family?

Doctor issues
- Why have you or your practice been selected?
- Workload already high and this patient could be high maintenance.
- Would you need to agree a contract with him?
- Be patient-centred.

Information gathering
- Contact previous GP – what are his feelings and wishes?
- Knowledge of reasons for relationship breakdown.
- Was there a possibility of a medical error?
- How demanding is the patient?
- Avoid judgement and respect colleagues.

Practice administration
- Should you interview the patient?
- Is your practice "closed' to new patients?
- Consider discussing at practice meeting.
- Are personal lists used in the practice?
- Nominate staff member to reply to request by letter or in person e.g. practice manager.

52. **"The homeless are being failed by the current system". In relation to the homeless, describe:**
  - **barriers to accessing health care;**
  - **specific health issues;**
  - **ways of delivering care.**

INTRODUCTION

Homelessness is a serious but difficult and multifactorial problem inextricable from the issues of poverty. For men aged 16–64 years, the risk of death in this group is 25 times that of the usual population.

ANSWER PLAN

Barriers to accessing health care
  - Difficulty registering with a GP – as a result many attend A&E instead sabotaging continuity of care and avoiding much-needed preventative interactions.
  - Poor attendance, motivation and failure of follow-up splinters chronic health care delivery.
  - Perceived wall of the "establishment" includes hospitals, housing agencies, police and even altruistic primary care doctors.
  - Actual prejudices and attitudes of all these workers may reinforce their opinion and provide real barriers.
  - Doctor's lack of expertise and feeling of hopelessness. It is very time consuming to start approaching all the aspects of the problem in an unmotivated group.
  - Homeless may not prioritize their health even though young men aged 16–29 sleeping rough have a death risk 40 times the national average.
  - May be heavy drinkers, smokers and drug users.
  - Patient's embarrassment and fear.
  - Lack of access to telephones/mail communication.

Specific health issues
  - More at risk from accidents, suicide, alcohol and drug related illness.
  - Poverty and squalor lead to high rates of illnesses such as skin conditions, gastroenteritis, asthma and a resurgence of TB.
  - High incidence of mental health disorders including schizophrenia, anxiety and depression.
  - High rates of violence and abuse.
  - Low life expectancy.
  - Poor compliance with treatment.
  - Homeless children face delayed development, lack education and face lifelong chronic ill health and social exclusion.

Delivering care

- Facilitate registering of the patients by using surgery address.
- Multiagency approach is required to balance health, education, housing and rehabilitation with assistance from relevant organizations e.g. the homeless person's charity Crisis.
- PMS has improved access for disadvantaged groups but there is an uneven spread across the country.
- Do you aim to offer a range of services to homeless people or work on reintegration to mainstream care to avoid further stigma?
- Potential role for nurse practitioners.
- Specific policy changes at governmental level?

RELEVANT LITERATURE

Developments in the provision of primary health care for homeless people. Lester, H et al., BJGP **52(2):** 91–92, 2002.
Preventing homelessness. Bandolier **45**: 3 Nov., 1997.

Evaluate the role and potential of the telephone with regard to the following.
- **NHS Direct.**
- **GP consultations.**

INTRODUCTION

This question requests evidence for the two major areas of primary care delivery. The telephone is likely to be an increasingly important, appropriate and acceptable means of patient contact.

ANSWER PLAN

NHS Direct
- In NHS Direct, nurses undertake triage with computer-aided support.
- High customer satisfaction but low usage by the elderly and ethnic minorities.
- Safe care – less than 1 in 220 000 calls led to adverse incidents in first 2 years.
- Seems to be meeting previously unrecognized demand in a group which already accesses health services.
- Unclear if NHS Direct can reduce need for immediate care services.
- The limited evidence suggests small significant decrease in out of hours GP calls.
- In one study over winter, the introduction of NHS Direct had no impact on the number of general practice consultations for respiratory infections (although this was not the primary aim of the service).
- Still unclear if service represents cost-effective care.
- Seems to be an expensive conduit to further health services.

General practice
- Use of telephone consultations for same-day appointments has been associated with time-saving but saving was offset by higher re-consultation and less use of opportunistic health promotion.
- In another study, telephone consultations reduced demand for face-to-face appointments with a GP by 39%. More than 92% of the telephone calls lasted less than 5 minutes. The telephone bill increased by 26%. For a substantial proportion of patients seeking same-day appointments telephone consultations were an acceptable alternative service.
- Telephone consultations enabled more people with asthma to be reviewed in briefer consultations with no apparent clinical disadvantage. Patients are satisfied with telephone consultations and this is likely to be a valuable way of reviewing asthmatics in the future.
- Expanded use can successfully involve organizing tests, discussing results and monitoring chronic problems which may help with achieving targets.
- The role of the telephone may be underused and is under-researched.

RELEVANT LITERATURE

Using telephones in primary care. Toon, P *BMJ* **324:** 1230–1231, 2002.

Telephone consultations to manage requests for same-day appointments: a randomised controlled trial in two practices. McKinstry, B *et al.*, *BJGP* **52(4):** 306–310, 2002.

The effect of GP telephone triage on numbers seeking same-day appointments. Jiwa, M *BJGP* **52(5):** 390–391, 2002.

Accessibility, acceptability, and effectiveness in primary care of routine telephone review of asthma: pragmatic, randomised controlled trial. Pinnock, H *et al.*, *BMJ* **326:** 477, 2003.

Impact of NHS Direct on demand for immediate care: observational study. Munro, J *BMJ* **321:** 150–153, 2000.

Impact of NHS Direct on general practice consultations during the winter of 1999–2000: analysis of routinely collected data. Chapman, R S *et al.*, *BMJ* **325:** 1397–1398, 2002.

NHS Direct audited. George, S *BMJ* **324:** 558–559, 2002.

54. A 75 year old man's last three blood pressure readings average 170/105. He has no other medical conditions and you consider him to be low risk. What is the basis of evidence for your choice of pharmacological treatment?

INTRODUCTION

A great deal of evidence supports the value of identifying and treating hypertension in the elderly population. This patient is a moderate/severe hypertensive.

ANSWER PLAN

Major trial evidence

- **EWPHE Trial (1985).** The European Working Party on Hypertension in the Elderly studied 840 patients >60 years old with thiazide medication vs. placebo and showed a significant reduction in cardiovascular mortality.
- **SHEP Trial (1991).** The Systolic Hypertension in the Elderly Project studied 4736 with isolated systolic hypertension (ISH) who were >60 years old. It compared thiazide to placebo showing a reduction in stroke, cardiovascular disease and mortality. Benefits extended to the over 80 age group with reductions in all major events. Treating ISH reduced CHD by 25%.
- **SYST-EUR (1997).** The Systolic Hypertension in Europe trial showed a strong benefit of treating ISH on end points of CV morbidity and mortality.
- **STOP–2 Trial (1999).** The Swedish Trial in Old Patients with Hypertension compared old and new drugs and showed similar advantages on BP and end points but was not sufficiently powered to decide on any difference between old drugs (thiazide and beta blocker) and new drugs (ACE inhibitors and calcium channel blockers).
- **Blood Pressure Lowering Treatment Trialists' Collaboration (2000).** Meta-analysis showed no major differences between older and newer agents.
- **ALLHAT (2002).** The largest ever randomized trial of antihypertensive treatment ($n = 42418 > 55$ years old) comparing diuretic, ACE inhibitor, calcium blocker and beta-blocker showed relative advantages for diuretic in terms of heart failure and stroke endpoints. They are at least as effective as more expensive treatments.

Guideline evidence

- Guidelines give a practical way of treating individuals e.g. SIGN guidelines.
- Target of < 140/90 mmHg.
- Assess risk e.g. using Joint British Societies Coronary Risk Prediction Chart

- An appropriate plan for this patient might be:
  - low dose thiazide diuretics as first line therapy;
  - beta-blockers or long-acting dihydropyridine calcium antagonists as alternative or supplementary therapy;
  - ACE inhibitors (or angiotensin II antagonists if cough) as alternative or supplementary therapy in the absence of renal artery stenosis;
  - alpha-blockers may be used as further supplementary therapy.

RELEVANT LITERATURE

British Hypertension Society guidelines for hypertension management: summary. *BMJ* **319**: 630–635, 1999.
Hypertension in Older People *SIGN Guideline 49.* Jan 2001.

55. Comment on the evidence for the following with relation to the treatment of low back pain in general practice.
   - **Use of medication.**
   - **Activity and exercise.**
   - **Psychosocial factors.**

INTRODUCTION

Back pain leads to 14 million GP consultations a year. Disability from back pain has increased fourfold since the late 1970s and cost estimates reach £6 billion.

ANSWER PLAN

Use of medication
A survey of GPs showed that optimal pain control is achieved in less than half of patients. Barriers include side effects, poor compliance and reluctance to prescribe.

Simple analgesics
- Paracetamol and paracetamol/weak opioid compounds taken regularly reduce low back pain.

NSAIDs
- Effective for short-term symptomatic relief of simple backache when prescribed at regular intervals.
- Different NSAIDs are equally effective.
- Less effective for the reduction of nerve root pain.
- Serious adverse effects particularly at high doses and in the elderly.

Muscle relaxants
- Effectively reduce acute back pain in the short-term.
- May have significant adverse effects including drowsiness and potential physical dependence even after a course as short as a week.

Strong opioids
- Appear to be no more effective in relieving low back pain symptoms than simpler analgesics.
- Significant adverse effects e.g. decreased reaction time, clouded judgement, drowsiness and potential physical dependence.

Activity and exercise

Bedrest
- Minimize bedrest and use for pain relief alone only if necessary.
- Bed rest for 2–7 days is worse than placebo or ordinary activity for relief of pain, rate of recovery, return to daily activities and days lost from work.

Normal activity

- Early return to normal physical activity leads to more rapid recovery, reduced chronic disability and less time off work.
- Use a "let-pain-be-your-guide" approach.
- Cochrane review showed advice to "stay active" has small beneficial effects for patients with acute simple low back pain, and little or no effect for patients with sciatica (but does no harm either).

Back exercises

- No more effective than no treatment initially.
- But may benefit those who have not returned to work at 6 weeks.
- Doubtful that specific back exercises produce improvement or that it is possible to select responders.

Manipulation

- Some may benefit from manipulation or mobilization by a trained physiotherapist or chiropractor.
- May allow short-term improvement in pain and activity levels.
- High patient satisfaction.
- Lack of evidence for case-selection, type of treatment or timing.

Psychosocial factors

Psychological factors (e.g. attitudes, beliefs about back pain, stress and depression), social factors (related to work and family) and biological factors are all important in chronicity of back pain.

- Eligibility for benefits is a predictor of persisting pain.
- Psychosocial factors influence response to treatment and rehabilitation at a much earlier stage than previously believed.
- They are more important risk factors for chronicity than biomedical symptoms and signs.
- Psychosocial "yellow flags" may predict poor outcomes and include belief that back pain is dangerous, fear-avoidance behaviour, tendency to low mood, social withdrawal and unrealistic expectations of treatment.
- Cochrane review concludes that intensive multidisciplinary biopsychosocial rehabilitation improves pain and function.

RELEVANT LITERATURE

Managing acute low back pain. *DTB* **36(12):** 64, 1998.
Clinical guidelines for the management of acute low back pain. RCGP, Updated 2001.
Systematic reviews of bed rest and advice to stay active for acute low back pain. Waddell, G *et al.*, BJGP **47:** 647–652, 1997.

56. A 19 year old girl attends with her boyfriend requesting emergency contraception 48 hours after an episode of unprotected intercourse. This is the third such request in a year. What are the issues for this consultation?

INTRODUCTION

This is a frequent problem in general practice. One third of 18–19 year old women have used postcoital contraception at least once over the preceding 2 years. It is not suitable for regular birth control.

FIVE POINT PLAN

Issues for the patient
- Beliefs about need for better contraception.
- Proper usage of current contraception.
- Is the partner here just for moral support?
- Embarrassment and fears over possible pregnancy, STDs.
- Any underlying agenda?

Issues for the doctor
- Why is the message not getting through?
- Self-awareness of irritation at time apparently wasted.
- Concentrate on finding common understanding.
- Own personal moral code or religious objections and requirement to refer to colleague if you feel unable to help.
- Need to sort out immediate clinical need.
- Need to remain accessible.

Consultation issues
- Ensure shared responsibility throughout.
- Decide if you wish to see patient alone or as couple.
- Aim to recruit understanding in partner as well.
- Take appropriate history e.g. reasons for repeated unprotected intercourse.
- Assess high-risk behaviour e.g. multiple partners, awareness of HIV, drug misuse.
- Careful explanation of treatment and written material.
- Good record-keeping.
- Explanation of treatment e.g. failure rate.
- Careful choice of future contraception.
- Safety net and follow-up.

Accessibility to teenagers
- Practice needs to remain accessible to younger patient groups.
- Other routes for treatment e.g. pharmacists, family planning clinics.
- Need to educate patients to make best use of all available resources.

Deregulation of emergency contraception

- Levonelle-2 was made available without prescription in the UK from pharmacies in January 2001.
- Available to over-16 year olds but costs about £25.
- Safe and effective at reducing unwanted pregnancy.
- Hopefully less stigma for patient as long as pharmacist has quiet area.
- Loses opportunity for further counselling and education.
- Some argue it should be free and will still save the NHS money and this has been tried in some areas.
- It is still available on prescription of course!

57. You call a practice meeting to suggest increasing your consultation time from 5 to 10 minute appointment slots. Your partners seem initially unhappy with this. Discuss.

INTRODUCTION

The traditional 5 minute time slot is disappearing. The increasing demands of delivering primary care necessitate an increased consultation time.

FIVE POINT PLAN

Benefits of longer consultations
- To realize the exceptional potential of the consultation.
- Increased patient satisfaction.
- Time to find psychological underpinnings.
- Time for opportunistic health care.
- Aids requirement for proper computer use.
- Better note-taking and housekeeping.
- May lower rates of re-attendance.
- Reduces stress levels in doctors.

Potential disadvantages
- Risk of overbooking.
- Extra workload may initially require more surgeries.
- Five minute appointments are more available.
- Implications for re-organization of the practice e.g. extra delegation.
- Patients may consult no less frequently.

Effect on practice
- Careful negotiating skills needed to bring other partners on board.
- Be prepared and examine objections.
- Need to encourage open debate and an initial trial.
- Discuss management of change.
- Receptionists will face initial reaction from patients, positive and negative.
- Need for future audit of success.

Effect on patients
- Should be a popular move in the long-term.
- Will increase wait for appointments initially.

Evidence points
- The demand for GP consultations is ever increasing.
- Nearly a fifth of patients are dissatisfied with the time allowed to them.
- More problems are identified in longer consultations.
- Longer consultations are more likely to include important elements of care but this may reflect doctor attributes as well.

- In one study, consultations denoting higher satisfaction appeared to patients to have lasted longer but actually did not implying it is more about quality time than actual time – doctor attributes again!
- Booking interval has not been shown to influence the time spent.
- Some research shows that longer consultations lead to fewer referrals and less prescribing.
- GPs on 5 minute appointments consistently run late, and have significantly more stress!
- Characteristics of patients have as much effect on consultation length as the characteristics of nationality and doctors combined.
- Consultations are longest for women patients seeing a GP in urban practices about psychosocial problems.

RELEVANT LITERATURE

Consultation length in general practice: a review. Wilson, A *BJGP* **41:**119–122, 1991.

Consultation length, patient-estimated consultation length, and satisfaction with the consultation. Cape, J *BJGP* **52(12):** 1004–1006, 2002.

The relationship between consultation length, process and outcomes in general practice: a systematic review. Wilson, A *et al.*, *BJGP* **52(12):** 1012–1020, 2002.

Consultation length in general practice: cross sectional study in six European countries. Deveugele, M *et al.*, *BMJ* **325:** 472, 2002.

58. Ben is 4 years old and has had no success with toilet training. Instead of using the potty, he regularly soils his clothes and the house. Conflict is arising in the household. His mother brings him and insists it has to stop. What are the important areas of this consultation?

INTRODUCTION

Soiling can be a symptom of turmoil in the child and a cause of turmoil in the household. A sensitive and considered approach is needed to reach the likely cause.

FIVE POINT PLAN

Parental agenda
- Explore mother's health beliefs and expectations.
- How is she coping?
- Possibility of a hidden agenda.

Doctor issues
- Need for empathy regarding the unpleasantness of the situation.
- Recognition of mother's anger.
- Self-awareness – "rather you than me". (*Don't say that!*).
- Sensitive approach to ease tension.
- Need for child-friendly approach and consultation room to observe interactivity of child.
- Need to manage own time efficiently.

Social issues
- Assess social circumstances e.g. role of father.
- Evaluate effect on the household.
- Presence of any changes or new stresses.
- Availability of support for the mother.
- Possibility of child abuse?

Primary Health Care Team
- All help gratefully received!
- Foster close relationship with local health visitor.
- Discussion with nursery teachers and/or community child health.

Management
- Probably no instant cure.
- Explore habits and routines, diet, timing of the problem.
- Examine old notes for other clues e.g. regular attendances.
- Relevant clinical examination and assessment of development.
- Develop differential diagnosis (e.g. constipation with overflow, behavioural response).
- Consider star chart for using the toilet.

- Start treatment plan e.g. laxative if suspicious of constipation.
- Consider referral for further management/behavioural approach as necessary.
- Plan next visit.

59. Discuss and evaluate interventions for smoking cessation in primary care in the following areas:
- **during the consultation;**
- **smoking cessation services;**
- **pharmaceutical approach.**

INTRODUCTION

Smoking is the most important avoidable health hazard. Smokers have a 50% chance of dying from their habit. Seventy per cent of smokers want to give up smoking.

ANSWER PLAN

During the consultation
- Use of the four As – Ask (about smoking at every opportunity), Advise (all smokers to stop), Assist (the smoker to stop), Arrange (follow-up).
- Screening questions – do you smoke? Do you want to stop? Do you want us to help?
- Referral to your nearest smoking cessation group or in-house programme.
- If insufficient motivation, offer encouragement and advice on benefits of stopping.
- Provide leaflet and leave the door open for the future.
- Need to be aware of time constraints.
- Brief advice at each encounter is highly cost-effective.
- Facilitate approach by maintaining readily accessible records on the current smoking status of patients.
- Specialist smokers' clinics should be the next point of referral for the motivated.

Smoking cessation services
- Specialist clinics or trained health care professionals e.g. practice nurses specializing in smoking cessation should be available.
- Both individual counselling and group therapy increase the chances of quitting to the same degree (but it is obviously cheaper in a group).
- Little evidence about the relative effectiveness of different psychological approaches e.g. aversive therapy.
- Valuable techniques include naming the day, removing temptation and enlisting support.
- Need to assess dependency and need for nicotine replacement therapies (NRT).
- Advise on the proven benefits of stopping e.g. excess risk of serious heart disease halved within a year of stopping.
- NICE guidance supports use of NRT and bupropion in appropriate cases
- self-help materials have no additional benefit over brief personal

advice. However, in 12 trials with no face to face contact, self help materials had a small effect when compared with no intervention.

- Individually tailored materials are more effective.
- Proactive telephone contact from a counsellor and reactive quitlines improve success rates cheaply.

Pharmaceutical approach

Nicotine replacement

- All of the different forms of NRT (gum, patch, nasal spray, inhaler and sublingual tablets/lozenges) are effective as part of a strategy. They increase quit rates approximately 1.5–2 fold.
- More intense levels of behavioural support and counselling further increase success e.g. doubles effect of brief GP advice to 20% quit rates.
- NRT is generally well tolerated, suitable only for motivated heavier smokers with evidence of nicotine dependence. Indiscriminate prescribing to unselected smokers is unlikely to be effective.

Other drugs

- Bupropion – efficacy may be even better than NRT. Research was performed in conjunction with counselling.
- Second-line medications, which are not approved for smoking cessation but have demonstrated some effectiveness, include clonidine, nortriptyline, mecamylamine, and lobeline.

Other approaches

- Acupuncture – no benefit compared with sham acupuncture. Benefit is likely to be a placebo effect. (Cochrane review).
- Hypnotherapy – trials found it no more effective than other behavioural interventions. It is difficult to evaluate in the absence of a sham procedure as a control (Cochrane review).

RELEVANT LITERATURE

Smoking Kills –a white paper on tobacco. Dept of Health, Dec 1998.
Effectiveness of interventions to help people stop smoking: findings from the Cochrane Library. Lancaster, T *et al*. (Cochrane Tobacco Addiction Review Group), *BMJ* **321**: 355–358, 2000.
Smoking cessation guidelines for health professionals: an update. West, R *et al*., *Thorax* **55**: 987–999, 2000.
Bupropion to aid smoking cessation. *DTB* **38(10)**: 80, Oct. 2000.

DEFINITION

Continuity of care lacks a clear definition but in it purest form is the tool of "personal doctoring". It has been a cornerstone of primary care but every major NHS reorganization has eroded it. Is this a tool we can afford to discard?

Some will argue that we can exchange continuity of care for continuity of information and records.

FIVE POINT PLAN

Advantages
- Time and use of review is the GP's most important tool. It requires continuity. (Beware the outrage of newspaper headlines – "I saw 16 doctors before I was diagnosed properly!". Of course. Each doctor was seen once!).
- Ongoing relationship facilitates disclosure by patients and helps to enable the patient.
- Accumulated knowledge allows understanding of social context over time.
- Doctor–patient relationship is in itself a therapeutic intervention.
- Develops own experience by seeing illness processes develop and hopefully recede.

Disadvantages of continuity
- Personal commitment from GPs (lifestyle advantages for GP in large practices).
- Reducing patient autonomy – does a personal list restrict patient choice?
- Costly to provide.
- Prevents GPs taking on other tasks e.g. management, teaching.
- Does not facilitate the fastest access to a GP.

Reasons for decline
- Development of group practices.
- Decline of personal lists.
- Use out-of-hours cooperatives and walk-in centres.
- Solutions for demand from better-informed, busy, impatient patients.
- Patients keen to seek out different health workers e.g. use of complementary therapies.

Evidence points
- In one survey 64% of patients rate a personal GP as very or extremely important.

- Reasonably strong and consistent association between visiting the same doctor and satisfaction for both patients and doctors.
- Satisfaction is also higher in practices that are small, non-training, or have personal lists.
- Some evidence points to improved intermediary outcomes e.g. compliance, uptake of preventative care, reduction in investigations and hospital admissions.
- Higher continuity develops higher levels of trust.
- A GP's sense of responsibility increases with the duration of the relationship and the number of contacts.
- However one-third stated continuity as moderately, slightly or not at all important.
- It is more highly valued for serious, psychological or family issues.
- For minor illness a personal doctor is much less important.

The future
- "If GPs really believe that it matters that a patient visits the same doctor, they need to ensure that this is taken into account in the development of primary care".
- GPs may need as individuals to decide which service they prefer to offer and so which practice to join.
- Hopefully a personal doctor will remain as an option (for the patients as well as the doctor) for those who wish to choose it.
- Demographic is becoming older and medicine more complex so continuity may become more important over time rather than less.

RELEVANT LITERATURE

Continuity of care – going out of style? Hjortdahl, P *BJGP* **51(9):** 699–700, 2001.
An exploration of the value of the personal doctor–patient relationship in general practice. Kearley, K *et al., BJGP* **51(9):** 712–718, 2001,
Does continuity in general practice really matter? Guthrie, B *et al., BMJ* **321:** 734–736, 2000.
Shaping tomorrow: issues facing general practice in the new millennium. *General Practitioner's Committee,* 2000.

61. You suggest at your weekly partners' meeting that a practice website would be a good idea. The idea is agreed but it seems you have inadvertently volunteered for the task.
  • How will you implement the plan?
  • What are the potential applications for the site?

INTRODUCTION

Most doctors now have a computer on their desk and many practices are expanding their IT exposure and developing websites.

ANSWER PLAN

Implementation of the plan

Where do we ideally want to be?
  • Involve the partners at each stage so they are engaged and have a stake in the idea.
  • What would everyone like the site to do?

How do we get there?
  • Formulate approach and agree aims/goals (solution engineering).
  • Use your skills of people management and good communication to negotiate agreement.
  • Be aware that old habits die hard and this could revolutionize procedures in the practice.
  • Prepare for a bereavement reaction from the senior partner!
  • Approach the problem as a business proposition.
  • Calculate cost – unlikely to be severe e.g. cost of software and web space.
  • Design pages, upload and advertise to potential users.
  • Facilitate discussion to avoid passive and active resistance along the way.

How do we know when we are there?
  • Is there a target date?
  • Decide on the first potential advantages and focus on them.
  • Audit success.

What are the potential benefits of the site?
  • Introduce staff and outline services.
  • Booking appointments on line.
  • Checking current appointments.
  • Resources for registrars.
  • Patient information – e.g. opening time, policies for clinics, information leaflets.
  • Patient education to allow using service more efficiently.

- Clinical information e.g. on minor illness, explanation about investigations.
- Illustrates a go-ahead "practice".
- Good learning experience for the practice.
- May be popular with patients.
- Consultation aid e.g. form to print out which assesses prostate symptoms score.
- Developing a website does not mean a need to enter into email consultations.

INTRODUCTION .

Eczema is a chronic condition and the most common form of inflammatory skin disease encountered in general practice. Approximately 25% of the population develops it at some time in their lives.

FIVE POINT PLAN

Patient-related issues
- How is the rash affecting her lifestyle and her psychological state?
- Problems of embarrassment in peer group and co-workers.
- Is it influencing personal relationships?
- What is her current use of treatment and knowledge of condition?
- Embarrassment seeing a fellow health worker?

Communication
- Sympathetic approach and skilled communication skills as this is a chronic condition.
- Have you had previous contact with this person as a patient or as a colleague?
- Avoid assumptions about the knowledge of health care worker.
- Explain. Reassure. Advise.
- Information leaflets and general advice may be of use e.g. from National Eczema Society.
- Back up with written information to ensure compliance.

Occupational issues
- Prejudices and society's ignorance can cause problems.
- Was she sent here by her work?
- Are the affected areas coverable e.g. use of gloves.
- Should she remain in a healthcare environment with an exposed possibly infected rash?
- Should her duties be revised for the time being?
- Would she like a sick note?

Diagnosis
- Do not assume this is eczema.
- Take appropriate history e.g. history of itchiness, atopy.
- Examination for relevant features e.g. distribution, scaling, vesicles, erythema, exudation.
- Is there secondary infection?
- Is this case manageable within general practice?

Therapeutics

General principles include:

- Keep the skin hydrated by the use of emollients.
- Avoid exacerbating factors e.g. soaps, detergents, irritating clothes (e.g. wool) and extremes of temperature.
- Treat exacerbations quickly with the appropriate strength of topical steroid.
- Treat secondary infection early with appropriate antibiotics and topical therapy.
- Consider use of new topical immunomodulators.
- Employ services of nurses if needed.
- Offer support, review and monitoring of progress.
- Awareness of criteria for referral e.g. for patch testing, diagnostic doubt or need for second-line therapies.

RELEVANT LITERATURE

Guidelines on the management of atopic eczema. *Primary Care Dermatology Society & British Association of Dermatologists, 2003.*

INTRODUCTION

This raises many issues of confidentiality, communication and consent.

FIVE POINT PLAN

Patient issues
- Is there an acceptable level of communication and understanding consistent with the Fraser ruling?
- Is there a preference to be seen alone?
- History of the problem.

Doctor self-awareness
- Discomfort with the consultation and need for examination.
- Need for clear understanding of patient's expectations.
- Is there preference for a female doctor?
- Impression of patient's competence to understand the issues.
- Need for a third party/friend/parent/health visitor/chaperone.

Consultation issues
- Need to develop suitable rapport and take time.
- Difficulties of dealing with teenagers e.g. need to reassure confidentiality.
- Establish sexual/relationship history including risk of sexually transmitted disease.
- Possibility of pregnancy.
- Contraceptive issues.
- Consider social context e.g. relationship with parents.
- Assessment of psychological state.
- Careful explanation and agreement of management.
- Need for medication or referral to paediatrician.
- Good record-keeping.

Legal and ethical issues
- Patient's right to confidentiality.
- Consent issues e.g. to examination.
- Possibility of non-consensual intercourse or incest.
- Discuss the need to inform other agencies versus respect for confidentiality.
- Awareness of possible action against doctor by parents.

Wider issues
- Making practice adolescent friendly and accessible.
- Education in local services that promote sexual health.
- Government policies for teenagers' sexual health.

64. **Jane Douglas is an intelligent 14 year old patient of yours whom you have been seeing regularly for the last 6 months. The specialist you referred her to has diagnosed chronic fatigue syndrome. What are the implications of this?**

INTRODUCTION

Chronic fatigue syndrome, known in the past as ME (myalgic encephalomyelitis), is a crippling but poorly understood disease. It is a complex mix of cerebral dysfunction and trigger factors. The GP may be the key professional involved in the management.

FIVE POINT PLAN

Issues for the patient

- Explore Jane's feelings and understanding of diagnosis.
- Know what advice has been given by specialist.
- Consider the psychological effects of the condition and label.
- The patient must be involved in all plans and decisions.

Issues for the doctor

- Personal knowledge and biases on the condition.
- Is this another name for MUPS?
- Need to encourage self-esteem in the patient.
- Non-dismissive and flexible approach.
- Show support for the family.
- Self-awareness e.g. feeling of impotence.

Educational and social issues

- Ongoing education is vital so need to encourage early return to school.
- Need for liaison with school.
- May need an educational tutor and a personal education plan.
- Consider the major psychological and practical impact on the family.

Diagnosis and treatment

- Are underlying causes excluded?
- Are you happy with the diagnosis?
- Awareness of the three main criteria – exercise-induced fatigue, psychoneurological disturbance (e.g. loss of concentration and memory) and fluctuations in severity of symptoms for longer than 6 months.
- Has there been appropriate advice given e.g. on pattern of disease, benefits available, on activity and intolerance of alcohol.
- Be cautious regarding medication.
- Monitor for anxiety and depression.
- Treatments of proven benefit are cognitive-behavioural therapy and graded exercise therapy.

Ongoing review

- Use of support agencies but encourage support from non-sufferers too for balance.
- Further information i.e. ME Association, Action for ME.
- Multidisciplinary team case reviews.
- Keep up to date with new developments.

RELEVANT LITERATURE

Review: behavioural interventions show the most promise for chronic fatigue syndrome. *EBM* **7:** 52, 2002.

INTRODUCTION

Several studies have shown that most patients with heart failure are not investigated and treated according to published guidelines. Reasons are complex and multifactorial. The main aim is for early access to echo to enable prescription of a life-extending ACE inhibitor.

FOUR POINT PLAN

Patient factors
- Immobility and the need for transport to facilities.
- Already taking ACE inhibitors and/or diuretics.
- Polypharmacy.
- Comorbidity.
- Old age and reduced life expectancy.

Doctor factors
- Knowledge – low awareness of research, false perception that other tests/clinical examination are sufficient.
- Communication – poor relationship with patient, concern over non-compliance.
- Skills – lack of clinical and interpretative skills.
- Diagnostic uncertainty concerned with heart failure and fear of undetected contraindications.
- Experience – lacking in experience of echo and ACE inhibitors, negative past experiences.
- Inertia – fatigue, reluctance to disturb the status quo (non-maleficence?).
- Judgement – decision to spare the elderly "stress".
- Rationing – doctor's false perception that benefit in elderly limited.
- Workload – of diagnosis, monitoring and follow-up e.g. renal biochemistry.

Pharmacological factors
- Overuse of diuretics as low-key "safe but inadequate" prescribing.
- Excessive concern over starting regime regarding first-dose hypotension although safe protocols are published.
- Concern over contraindications and side effects of ACE inhibitors.
- Evidence shows appropriate uptake of ACE inhibitors < 50 % but tolerance up to 90%.

Organizational factors
- Lack of access (especially open-access) to echo.
- Teamwork – reluctance of local cardiologists.

- Practice issues – lack of guidelines and agreed policy, slow implementation of new research, lack of involvement of practice nurse to facilitate chronic review.
- Cost of echo and prescribing expense of ACE inhibitors (even though cost-effective treatment).
- Relationships between primary and secondary care influence how general practitioners manage heart failure.

RELEVANT LITERATURE

The barriers to effective management of heart failure in general practice. Hickling, J A et al., BJGP 51(8): 615–618, 2001.
Barriers to accurate diagnosis and effective management of heart failure in primary care: qualitative study. Fuat, A et al., BMJ 326:196, 2003.

INTRODUCTION

What is a GP? Perhaps a "licenced medical graduate who gives personal, primary and continuing care to individuals, families and a practice population irrespective of age, sex and illness". The GP tries to understand disease at a community level and aims to optimise use of healthcare resources. Defining a good one is tough.

FIVE POINT PLAN

Personal qualities
- Approachability, non-discriminatory and non-judgemental manner.
- Good communication skills in terms of listening, language used and cultural sensitivity.
- Accessible in terms of consultation time/duration, visiting, telephone advice/availability.
- Be up-to-date.
- Confident but recognize limitations.
- Confidentiality and trustworthiness.
- Efficient in terms of documents, referrals and follow up.

Professional qualities
- Technically competent and registered appropriately.
- Appropriately experienced.
- Safe selection/recruitment process – references/police checks.
- Willingness to undertake professional self-development and support team development.
- Team player and supportive of rest of team/appreciation of the role of others.
- Good leadership and self-analytical skills.
- Good time-management skills.
- Ability to manage and support change.
- Approachable, enthusiastic, innovative and forward thinking.
- Support and engage with patient participation groups.

Measures to monitor these qualities
- Use of audit.
- Adherence to policies, protocols and codes of practice.
- Performance review and appraisal.
- Complaints procedures and compliments.
- Critical incident analysis.
- Prescribing data.
- Waiting times.
- Patient satisfaction.

- Revalidation, consultation satisfaction rating, or the "fellowship by assessment" quality assurance programme of the RCGP.
- Assessments by the Commission for Health Improvement and star ratings.

Difficulties of measurement
- Can demoralize staff and distort behaviour.
- Measures of quality can be misapplied and abused.
- No such thing as the perfect measure – can result in perverse incentives or lead to data manipulation.
- Lack of standards to compare data to.
- Measures can be perceived as capricious tools for shifting responsibility and blame.

Why measure?
- Patients, funders, commissioners, provider organizations, and health professionals want to know how "good" are individual doctors, teams, and healthcare organizations.
- Crucial for a range of purposes – such as learning, quality improvement, accountability, and regulation.
- To facilitate safety, value for money healthcare and effective change.
- To protect themselves from the bad and incompetent.

RELEVANT LITERATURE

Measuring "goodness" in individuals and healthcare systems. Pringle, M *et al.*, *BMJ* **325:** 704–707, 2002.
Quality at general practice consultations: cross-sectional survey. Howie, J G R *et al.*, *BMJ* **319:** 738–743, 1999.

INTRODUCTION

The recent completion of the human genome project and current research will lead to the identification of new risk factors for common diseases such as cardiovascular disease, diabetes, and cancers. Clinical genetics departments will be overstretched and primary care workers will be required to advise patients about genetic issues.

FIVE POINT PLAN

Role of the GP

- Well-placed to support genetic medicine given the focus on the family and computerized longitudinal health records.
- UK GPs tend to accept role as a legitimate part of primary care.
- Provision of basic genetics information to help understanding and informed decision making.
- Need to identify and refer individuals who may benefit from genetic services.
- Development of new skills in assessing genetic risk e.g. adequate family history and forming a pedigree.
- Recognition of common patterns of inheritance and awareness of specific familial cancers.
- Awareness of the importance of ethnicity in determining risk.
- Communication of risk and counselling in a non-directive manner.
- Monitor and co-ordinate health of individuals with a genetic disorder.
- Psychosocial support for an affected family.
- Understand limitations of genetic testing, including the organizational implications of testing for insurance.

Organizational implications

- Multifaceted team approach is required.
- Community genetic counsellors could act as outreach workers from the genetics clinic to liaise with local GPs.
- PCGs could support development of a primary care specialist as an intermediate point of referral.
- Educational programmes e.g. basic genetic counselling training for doctors.
- Use of computerized decision support software.
- Use of community groups to address individual needs.

Future possibilities

- Currently the most important elements for primary care are prediction of risk of certain cancers and carrier screening for common autosomal recessive conditions such as cystic fibrosis.

- Infinite possibilities for screening and diagnosis.
- Predispositional testing could predict risk of common conditions such as diabetes and cardiovascular disease.
- Pharmacogenetics could explain individual variation in drug response and be used to identify patients at risk of severe adverse effects from drugs e.g. bleeding complications of warfarin or non-response.

Ethical/legal considerations and controversies
- Widespread issues e.g. screening, prenatal testing, presymptomatic testing
- Use of predictive tests is also limited by absence of treatment.
- Discrimination issues (insurance coverage, employment).
- Informed consent for testing.
- Paternity determinations.
- Potential harm from inappropriate use of genetic testing.

Resource issues
- Ever increasing patient demand as new tests and associations are discovered.
- Limited number of professionals trained in genetics.
- Inevitable need for expansion of integrated services and related costs.

RELEVANT LITERATURE

The challenge of integrating genetic medicine into primary care. Emery, J *et al.*, *BMJ* **322**:1027–1030, 2001.

68. **Anna is a 14 year old girl who attends with her 25 year old boyfriend. He asks you to prescribe the oral contraceptive pill as they are planning on sleeping together. The families are personal friends of yours. What issues are raised?**

INTRODUCTION

The UK has the highest teenage pregnancy rate in Western Europe. At present 19% of women start sexual intercourse before the age of 16.

FIVE POINT PLAN

Patient issues
- Is she feeling pressured by her older boyfriend?
- Explore Anna's feelings, knowledge and understanding.
- Possible embarrassment about presenting.
- Presence of adequate level of maturity?

Issues for the doctor
- Awareness of own feelings about this relationship.
- Potential conflict of interests as you know the family.
- Concern over the large age gap and greater experience of boyfriend.
- You need to talk to Anna alone.
- Encourage her to talk to parents and perhaps return to see you with them.
- The need to be able to justify your actions before the GMC.
- Can you help avoid an unwanted pregnancy in a schoolgirl?

Use of the consultation
- There is a lot to get through and they may default at follow-up.
- Sympathetic and non-judgemental manner.
- Extremely important to gain rapport.
- Take the opportunity to encourage a sense of self-confidence and personal worth.
- Appropriate medical history and examination as for any such prescription.
- Explain risk of HIV, STD and relationship between early intercourse and cervical dysplasia.
- Emphasize that she informs her parents and explore why she may be reticent.
- Offer to talk to parents on her behalf.

Legal and confidentiality issues
- What is proposed is technically rape even if she consents.
- Has abuse already taken place? The right of confidentiality must be balanced against the protection of vulnerable people from serious harm.

- Warn the boyfriend he is about to break the law.
- Reassure Anna of your duty of confidentiality.
- Patient's concern about confidentiality is the main deterrent to asking for contraception. (Nearly 75% of girls < 16 years fear GPs would not guarantee confidentiality.)
- Fraser guidelines: girl <16 years can be prescribed contraception without parental consent providing her understanding/intelligence is sufficient to allow consent, you encourage her to inform a parent and contraception is in her best interests.

Management plan
- Act in Anna's best interests.
- Justify your decision regarding the prescription being aware that intercourse is likely still to occur.
- If you feel unable to agree you must refer to a colleague or advisory service with different views e.g. Brook Youth Advisory Centres.
- You may feel she needs further counselling about the psychological and physical implications.
- Offer follow-up.

INTRODUCTION

Non-concordance, or non-compliance, may be voluntary or unintentional but is estimated to contribute to therapeutic failure in about 50% of prescribing. It represents a major clinical challenge.

THREE POINT PLAN

Causes
Many of these stem from a breakdown in communication and relate more to the patient's agenda than the doctor's.
- Failure to understand patent's beliefs about illness.
- Impact on patient's life e.g. drug doses too frequent or too many drugs.
- Side-effects unacceptable.
- Patient not sufficiently involved in decision to prescribe.
- Quality of the doctor–patient relationship.
- Doctor's manner e.g. lack of effect or showing uncertainty about when to end HRT.
- Overprescription.
- Lack of time and opportunity/encouragement to ask questions.
- Incomplete advice from doctor or pharmacist.
- Financial – unable to afford prescription.
- Cultural or religious barriers.
- Age – older, more vulnerable patients more likely to hoard medications.

Consequences
- Loss of benefit.
- Failure to hit primary care targets e.g. undermining of antihypertensive targets.
- Impaired prevention strategies for heart disease and strokes.
- Waste of resources – unnecessary additional drugs prescribed.
- Unexpected withdrawal effects.

Solutions
- Methods of checking compliance (questioning, counting tablets, measuring blood levels).
- Communication issues – staying patient-centred while becoming evidence-based.
- Use simple language and repeat important messages.
- Tailor prescribing e.g. modified-release drugs, shorter courses of treatment.
- Clear verbal and written instructions.

- Review medications periodically and feedback to patient (and relatives if available).

RELEVANT LITERATURE

Primary non-compliance with prescribed medication in primary care. Beardon, P *et al.*, *BMJ* **307:** 846–848, 1993.
Why treatments fail. *DTB* **36(6):** 31, 1998.

USEFUL WEBSITE

www.medicines-partnership.org

70. Discuss the evidence regarding the use of lipid-lowering drugs in general practice.

INTRODUCTION

Despite proven benefits and guidance from the NHS's National Service Framework for Coronary Heart Disease, statins are still under-prescribed despite a wealth of classic evidence that illustrates effectiveness.

EVIDENCE

Primary prevention

WOSCOPS (1995)

- The West of Scotland Primary Prevention Study involved 6595 males aged 45–65 with total cholesterol above 6.5 mmol/l but no history of CHD who took pravastatin or placebo for 5 years.
- *Key results*: Total cholesterol decreased by 20% and death from coronary heart disease by 31%. Treating 1000 patients for 5 years would prevent 7 deaths from CHD and 20 non-fatal MIs.

AFCAPS/TexCAPS (1998)

- The Air Force/Texas Coronary Atherosclerosis Prevention Study involved men and women with average cholesterol levels who took lovastatin or placebo for 5.2 years.
- *Key results:* New CV disease was reduced by 54% in women and 34% in men
- The starting point for prevention is CHD event risk.
- Those at highest risk of CHD events have most to gain by treatment.
- Cholesterol level alone is a poor predictor of risk.
- Absolute rather than relative risk reduction gives a better estimate of the benefits of lipid-lowering drug treatment.
- Statins should be considered for primary prevention when the 10 year risk of a major coronary event is ≥30% using the Joint British Chart.

Secondary prevention

The 4S trial (1994)

- The Scandinavian Simvastatin Survival Study involved 4444 patients (81% were men) between 35 and 70 years with known ischaemic heart disease and total cholesterol of 5.5–8.0 mmol/l given simvastatin or placebo over 5.4 years.
- *Key results*: A lowering of total cholesterol by 20% was produced. This gave a reduction in total mortality by 30% and in coronary deaths by 42%.

CARE (1996)

- The Cholesterol and Recurrent Event study involved 4159 post-MI patients under 75 with a total cholesterol under 6.2 mmol/l. It was a 5 year study of pravastatin vs. placebo.
- *Key results*: Secondary prevention was shown to be effective in lower/average ranges of cholesterol. Fatal and non-fatal cardiac events were reduced by 24% and stroke by 28%.

LIPID (1998)

- The Long-term Intervention with Pravastatin in Ischaemic Disease Study Group was similar to CARE using 9014 patients with unstable angina or post MI under 75 with cholesterol below 7 mmol/l.
- *Key results*: Fatal and non-fatal cardiac events were reduced by 24% and overall mortality by 22%.
- Secondary prevention has been shown to be highly cost-effective at £5000 per life year saved using simvastatin. As cost falls, cost-effective thresholds may fall.
- Approaches for secondary prevention depend on current protocols e.g. SIGN guidelines have a target of total cholesterol <5.0 mmol/l.

Future developments

- The Heart Protection Study (2002) was a 5 year placebo-controlled study of 20 536 which recently showed that simvastatin 40 mg reduced MI and stroke by about one-third even in patients with normal or low cholesterol. They concluded any patient with a risk factor e.g. diabetes should be on a statin tripling the number of candidates for statins. At the time of writing, guidance is awaited on the cost implications.
- Unpublished research has shown a 79% reduction in Alzheimer's disease (*BMJ* **324:** 936, 2002)
- Another study has shown a large reduction in macular degeneration in the statin group over 5 years (*BMJ* **323:** 375–376, 2001)

71. Mrs Barker brings her 6 year old son Matthew who has had a temperature of 39.5°C and been vomiting in the night. He has also been complaining of earache and she has given him some ibuprofen to ease the pain. You are fairly certain this is an acute otitis media.
Comment on:
• Influences on the dynamics of this consultation.
• Your options for clinical management.

INTRODUCTION

This is a common clinical problem with one in four children under ten reporting such an episode.

ANSWER PLAN

Factor influencing the dynamics

Patient factors
• Be aware of mother's concerns and personal experience of raising a child.
• There are two patients who need "treatment".
• Parental expectation of antibiotics – often spending time on reassurance is more valuable.
• Trust in doctor.

Doctor factors
• Need to gain rapport and mutual trust with mother and child.
• Use techniques that adopt child-friendly approach e.g. use of play.
• Paediatric experience and familiarity with good examination skills.
• Employ mother to aid good examination.
• Do you have previous knowledge of this family that helps you in the doctor–patient relationship?
• Awareness of social circumstances.
• Awareness that prescription for self-limiting conditions may increase future expectations.

Clinical management
• Consider other diagnoses if not certain about AOM e.g. meningitis, urinary tract infection (UTI).
• Usually a self-limiting condition unless there are risk factors for a poor outcome.
• Antibiotics are widely debated but have a limited role despite over prescription in the UK. Aim to use sparingly in AOM. They double risk of diarrhoea, vomiting and rash.
• SIGN Guidelines exist to aid management. Validated factors that may indicate benefit of antibiotics include high temperature and vomiting.
• Recommended symptomatic treatment is paracetamol first-line.

- Initially avoid ibuprofen due to side-effect profile.
- Options are:
  - prescribe antibiotics (early use may improve symptoms quicker if risk factors exist);
  - do not prescribe antibiotics (most AOM ultimately self-limiting);
  - give a deferred prescription for antibiotics (a compromise which empowers parents and reduces use of antibiotics).

In Matthew's case, in view of the systemic symptoms, treatment with a broad spectrum antibiotic such as amoxicillin would be justified. This may shorten symptoms, particularly pain, between days 2 and 7. There is no benefit in the first 24 hours.

Alternatively, giving a prescription and using a wait-and-see approach for 72 hours can reduce use of antibiotics by 76% and merit parental satisfaction.
- Arrange review.

RELEVANT LITERATURE

Diagnosis and management of childhood otitis media in primary care. SIGN Guideline 66. Feb 2003.
Predictors of poor outcome and benefits from antibiotics in children with acute otitis media: pragmatic randomised trial. Little, P et al., BMJ 325:22, 2002.
Are antibiotics indicated as initial treatment for children with acute otitis media? A meta-analysis. Del Mar, C B et al., BMJ 314:1526, 1997.

INTRODUCTION

Health related websites contain some of the most accessed information on the web.

THREE POINT PLAN

Use by patient
- Simple, accessible from home, easy to use.
- Broadens access to information – can become very well-informed.
- An important aspect of self-care.
- Enables access to patient support pages and groups.
- Use of email consultations.
- Use as a second opinion.
- Use to access own practice for information, appointments etc.

Implications for medical professionals
- Perception of a threat – "the new newspaper clipping is a printout from the Net".
- Fantastic resource for information e.g. free BMJ where rapid responses enable professional dialogue.
- Facilitates research e.g. free Medline.
- Reduces need for paper information.
- Medical professionals can also be misled by unreliable information.
- Use in the consultation e.g. information on medication.
- Use of a practice website.
- Use of NHS net to co-ordinate healthcare professionals.
- Loss of continuity e.g. competing with an opinion from an on-line doctor.

Concerns
- Lack of regulation and reliability of information (European Commission aims to publish code of good practice).
- False health claims made and many new "alternative therapies" are peddled.
- Information not always relevant to UK health system.
- Offering email advice still bears medico-legal responsibilities and some UK doctors have recently been disciplined by the GMC.
- Much more research is needed to optimize use of the "infinite potential".

RELEVANT LITERATURE

The quality of health information on the internet. Purcell, G P et al., BMJ **324:** 557–558, 2002.

INTRODUCTION

The development of a new role of medical assistant or physician's assistants has a strong lobby of support for use in hospitals to replace part of the junior doctor's role. They may also have a role in general practice.

FIVE POINT PLAN

Role of the PA
- A highly trained professional in his/her own right.
- But intermediate role unevaluated in UK care.
- Shown to be a useful adjunct in the US.
- Could help to meet practice targets.
- A mid-level practitioner who may not be useful for "nursing" tasks.
- Lifestyle advantage for PA of office-hours only workload.

Patient care
- US model shows high productivity and patient satisfaction.
- Needs awareness of the UK system.
- Requires education of patients about the role.
- As in nurse practitioner research, the extra time spent should create satisfaction.

Issues for the practice
- What skills are on offer? Is training and function too generic or is the flexibility valuable?
- Valuable new learning experience for the practice.
- May save doctor time.
- Need to guarantee safety of patients.
- Vigilance and supervision needed.
- Care in delegating appropriate tasks (PA may not be an independent practitioner).
- Need to develop protocols.
- Extra work to supervise and train PA, who could be the first contact in minor illness and injury.
- Opposition of partners to non-physicians providing medical care, especially diagnosis and treatment.
- Relationship with practice nurse. (US models have shown antagonism with nursing profession.)
- Programme of revalidation in place?

Resources issues
- Recruitment and retention problems in the NHS need new solutions.
- A new grade may be required to plug gaps in service – a radical solution in need of a pilot study?
- Will this approach be cost-effective? PAs in the US have a higher starting salary than doctors (average $57 700).
- Lengthy expensive training – is it better to train more doctors and focus efforts to increase recruitment to general practice.

Long-term issues
- What will be the long-term impact of a new grade?
- Competition with nurse practitioners?
- Need for accredited educational programmes.
- Professional indemnity issues.
- Issues of referral and prescribing privileges.

RELEVANT LITERATURE

The physician assistant: would the US model meet the needs of the NHS?
Hutchinson, L, *BMJ* **323:** 1244, 2001.

INTRODUCTION

The NHS Cervical Screening Programme tested for precancerous change in 3.2 million women in 2001–2002 when 5-year coverage reached 81.6%. GPs should encourage women between 20 and 64 years to attend when called, usually every 3 years. The programme has been successful and mortality rates are continuing to fall.

FOUR POINT PLAN

Patient factors
- Assess health beliefs and knowledge of the importance of the programme.
- Reasons for defaulting – failure of the system or anxiety?
- History of prior experience or other concerns.

GP approach
- Treat presenting complaint appropriately.
- Sensitive approach, avoid pestering.
- Express concern over possible risk, requirement to inform about the programme.
- Inform patient and correct any misconceptions.
- Careful explanation of need to detect changes before cancer occurs.
- Reassure about privacy, use of chaperone etc.
- Respect final fully informed decision.
- Opportunistic advice e.g. smoking, need for contraception.
- Keep good records of decision made.

Organizational issues
- Importance of improving coverage and hitting targets.
- Follow up non-responders – why has this patient slipped through the net?
- Need for appropriate audit to avoid this.
- Role of opportunistic screening.
- Availability of female nurse or doctor.
- Availability of chaperones to minimize patient's anxiety.
- Further advice about risk factors could be a role for a well-woman clinic.
- Liaison with PCO which runs the call and recall service and results notification.

Future developments

- Future possibilities include reduction to 5 year screening. A *BJGP* Discussion paper in June 2002 suggested that too many women are screened too frequently and that to be cost-effective the screening interval should increase to 5 years and routine screening restricted to women aged 25–50 years while still recruiting those that have never been screened.
- Resources should then be targeted at improving the quality of the service.
- Use of future tests – liquid-based cytology and human papilloma virus testing are being evaluated.
- The HART Trial (HPV in Addition to Routine Testing) involves 12 000 women aged between 30 and 60 and is assessing HPV testing. It has potential to save money by increasing the screening interval or eventually replacing cytology but currently detects too many false positives due to high sensitivity.

RELEVANT LITERATURE

Cervical Screening Programme Annual Review. 2002.
How can we develop a cost-effective quality cervical screening programme? Wilson S, *et al.*, BJGP **52(6):** 485–490, 2002.

INTRODUCTION

The prevalence of obesity in children in increasing. It is a chronic condition that will have increasing resource implications for primary care.

FIVE POINT PLAN

Patient-centred approach
- Any underlying problems e.g. bullying, bereavement, self-esteem issues.
- Reason for attending now.
- Assessment of psychological status of child and mother.
- Does Paul see his weight as a problem?
- Where did she hear of this medication? What are her expectations of it and you?
- Need for sensitive communication skills especially as she will not be leaving with what she ostensibly came in for.
- Is mother obese as well? What efforts has she made so far?

Self-awareness of the doctor
- Difficult, time-consuming territory.
- Cynicism about the efficacy of treatments.
- Perceived non-compliance of patients.
- Lack of training in counselling and motivating patients to change their behaviour.
- Need to avoid stigmatising and blaming patients for their obesity.
- Lack of personal knowledge and confidence in managing morbid obesity.
- Acknowledgement of any personal prejudice.

Practice issues
- Increasingly frequent, time-consuming consult.
- Time management issues for the practice.
- Are self-help leaflets available?
- Can the practice nurses help in monitoring and encouragement?
- Would an obesity clinic be feasible?
- Can you offer a team-based approach e.g. access to dietician?

Clinical aspects
- Exclude secondary causes of obesity.
- Awareness of orlistat and NICE guidelines, which Paul is unlikely to meet.
- Manufacturer does not support use in children.
- Awareness of local resources to give support.

- Who else can you involve?
- Evidence suggests most people can be helped to manage their weight aiming for a gradual weight loss of 5–10% of initial body weight by caloric restriction, increased physical activity, and behaviour therapy. Small improvement can have large effect on primary care health targets.
- Be positive, suggest initial advice e.g. a food diary, exercise and healthy eating and plan review.

Broader issues
- Should the NHS foot the bill for drugs such as orlistat or prioritize resources elsewhere?
- How can PCTs help target the epidemic of obesity effectively with locally funded programmes?
- Responsibility of media which reinforce stereotypes of thin people.
- Existence of local patient support groups and facilities for exercise.
- Is obesity really a medical problem?

RELEVANT LITERATURE

An approach to weight management in children and adolescents in primary care.
National Obesity Forum, 2002.

76. "The Department of Health has said it has yet to determine whether the best screening tool would be flexible sigmoidoscopy or faecal occult blood testing." Evaluate the evidence for these strategies in normal risk individuals.

INTRODUCTION

Colorectal cancer is the second most common cancer fatality with 30 000 new cases per year in the UK and an overall 5-year survival of 40%.

The disease is a good candidate for screening. Intervention does improve outcome but a truly appropriate cost-effective approach is awaited in the UK.

Several countries have screening programmes. The American Cancer Society recommends an annual digital rectal examination for people aged over 40, an annual faecal occult blood (FOB) test for people aged over 50, and flexible sigmoidoscopy every 3–5 years for people aged over 50.

Cost and use of already strained resources are a concern in the UK and results from large trials are awaited.

ANSWER PLAN

Faecal occult blood
- Cheap, safe, easy and detects blood from high in GI tract.
- Reasonably acceptable and non-invasive.
- Compliance is around 38%, but education might improve this.
- Low sensitivity for colorectal neoplasia with about 40% of cancers missed by a single screen, leads to the need for repeat FOBs. Cancers bleed only intermittently giving false negative results and bleeding is a late stage.
- False positive results can occur due to diet e.g. red meat.
- Three large randomized trials have convincingly shown that FOB testing can reduce mortality from colorectal cancer by about 15%.
- Annual or biennial FOB screening also reduces the incidence of colorectal cancer by up to 20%.
- Approximately 2% of the normal risk population will have positive results but 89% will not have cancer and the subsequent tests are relatively invasive. One in 10 will have cancer and one in three will have adenoma.

Flexible sigmoidoscopy
- It is quick, highly sensitive and specific.
- Is an investigation and treatment combined.
- Invasive, operator-dependent and may be unacceptable to patients.
- More expensive than rigid sigmoidoscopy but less uncomfortable for patients and has much higher yield.
- Many nurses are now trained to perform flexible sigmoidoscopy, making potential screening programmes using this technique more cost-effective.

- Uptake is likely to be around 45% and of these 6% will subsequently need full colonoscopy.
- Fails to detect at least 25% of significant adenomas.
- Evidence suggests single flexible sigmoidoscopy at the end of the sixth decade is a cost-effective, acceptable way of preventing 3500 deaths.
- May be a better initial test than FOBs as estimates say it could reduce mortality in those tested by 35%.
- Polypectomy after rigid sigmoidoscopy reduces the chance of rectal cancer as much as 30 years later.
- Once-only flexible sigmoidoscopy presents a promising alternative to FOBs, but awaits results of a current multicentred RCT looking at effect on incidence and mortality in an asymptomatic population aged under 65.

RELEVANT LITERATURE

Colorectal cancer screening in the UK: joint position statement by the British Society of Gastroenterology, the Royal College of Physicians, and the Association of Coloproctology of Great Britain and Ireland. *Gut* **46:** 746–748, 2000.
ABC of colorectal cancer: Screening. Scholefield, J H *BMJ* **321:** 1004–1006, 2000.

77. Antihypertensive therapy is of particular importance in type 2 diabetics. What evidence is there to support this statement?

INTRODUCTION

Hypertension is a common and potent risk factor for vascular disease in diabetics. The clinical benefits of aggressive treatment are now clear but two-thirds need two or more agents and one-third need at least three.

ANSWER PLAN

General evidence
- More than 70% of type 2 diabetics are hypertensive.
- Hypertension frequently precedes the diagnosis of diabetes and shares similar risk factors e.g. obesity.
- It increases risk of coronary heart disease by 2–3 times and of heart failure by 5 times.
- Non-pharmacological interventions are useful e.g. smoking cessation, exercise, diet but most will need medication.
- Each 10 mmHg reduction in systolic pressure is associated with a 15% reduction in the risk of cardiovascular death over 10 years.
- Thiazides, beta-blockers, ACE inhibitors and calcium channel blockers are all effective in lowering BP and reducing the risk of cardiovascular events.
- ACE inhibitors should be considered as first-line therapy in patients with microalbuminuria due to their additional benefit on renal function.

Specific evidence
(The major trials used a variety of agents to achieve BP control).
- UKPDS – The UK Prospective Diabetes Study (1998)
  (n=1148 all type 2 diabetics). The major embedded study in this group was related to BP control. Follow up over 8 years showed that a modest reduction in BP by 10/5 mmHg was associated with major reduction in risks of stroke, heart failure, coronary heart disease and all diabetic end-points. There may even be more benefit from control of BP than of glucose.
- SHEP – The Systolic Hypertension in the Elderly Programme (1991)
  (n=4736, diabetic n =583). This showed greater benefit of hypertensive control in the diabetic sub-group.
- HOT – Hypertension Optimal Treatment trial (1998).
  (n=18790, diabetic n=1501). The Hypertension Optimal Treatment trial showed 51% reduction in major cardiovascular events in diabetics with an intensive approach to a diastolic target of 80 mmHg.
- SYST-EUR (1997)
  (n=4695, diabetic n=492). This found that with adequate antihypertensive treatment the excess risk of diabetes was almost completely elimi-

nated with approximately 70% reductions in cardiovascular mortality and all cardiovascular end-points.

- Summary of more recent trials:

HOPE (2000) The Heart Outcome Prevention Evaluation study showed independent vascular protective and renoprotective effects with an ACE inhibitor (ramipril).

LIFE (2002) This trial used losartan versus atenolol with add-on thiazide in high-risk hypertensives including diabetics. BP reduction was similar but a further benefit of the angiotensin receptor blocker was a 25% risk reduction in stroke.

ALLHAT (2002) showed that benefit of thiazides outweighed any worries about impact on glucose levels.

RELEVANT LITERATURE

Management of Diabetes. *SIGN Guideline No 55.*

INTRODUCTION

The GP is ideally placed for pre-test HIV discussion. The recent National Strategy for Sexual Health and HIV Implementation Plan aims to increase the role of primary care in testing.

FIVE POINT PLAN

Patient's reasons
- Ask about main concerns and reasons for presenting now.
- Check understanding that it is a test for HIV rather than AIDS.
- Is there an underlying agenda?

Consultation aims
- Identify risk activity.
- Consider the patient's sexual relationships.
- Take a related history including travel, drug use, occupation.
- Consider hepatitis B immune status.
- Discuss pros and cons of testing.
- Discuss the impact of a positive test.
- Is there an underlying psychological problem?
- Explain the procedure.
- Suitable recording of salient aspects.
- Arrange appointment to discuss results.

Consent and confidentiality issues
- Make certain of obtaining informed consent e.g. ask the patient to summarize or repeat salient points.
- Confirm he wants to go ahead.
- Ensure confidentiality e.g. coded labeling of samples.
- Avoid giving results over the phone.
- In the event of a positive test, avoid a breach of confidentiality by explaining the importance of informing relevant colleagues.

Issues for the practice
- Is written material available?
- Ensure failsafe follow-up of positive results
- The need to develop a protocol.
- Future role in increasing public's awareness of testing.

Related issues
- GUM clinics offer an open access for confidential HIV testing.
- Increasing training and education for GPs will help to promote and support testing.

- Many concerns have centred around insurance consequences. GMC guidance invites GPs to discuss information required on forms before filling them in and allow patients to see the form before submission.
- Advice from the Association of British Insurers and the BMA states that only positive tests will affect insurance.

RELEVANT LITERATURE

Guidelines for pre-test discussion on HIV testing. *Dept of Health* 1996.
Serious communicable diseases. *General Medical Council* 1997.
The National Strategy for Sexual Health and HIV. *Dept of Health* 2001.

INTRODUCTION

Extended role nursing is an increasing area and may benefit a practice in a variety of ways in the future.

FIVE POINT PLAN

Nurse issues
- Will be good for the nurse – acquiring skills helps increase motivation.
- Increases awareness of different skills required between doctors and nurses.
- What are her reasons for deciding this at this stage? Might she have a second agenda?

Effect on partners
- Reluctance on the part of the partners to release nurse.
- May feel threatened.
- How will decision be made?
- Important to appear positive and encourage staff.
- May depend on nurse's length of service and relationship with the practice.
- Likely to increase work for all the partners in the short-term.
- Unlikely to reduce GP workload long-term but the case shift may be advantageous.
- One nominated supervisor in the short-term may even need to attend parts of her course with her.
- Initial training will mean she sees work of the partners at close range.

Effect on the practice
- Has she convinced you her new skills will benefit the practice and patients?
- Improves accessibility – new service is likely to be acceptable for those that choose it.
- May be able to see more minor illness freeing GP time for more complex cases.
- May aid or indeed cause GPs to specialise more.
- Training paves way for future extended roles e.g. in chronic disease clinics.
- But after training she could takes her skills elsewhere.
- What are the consequences of refusing e.g. disappointment or resignation?
- May impair continuity of care.
- Costs of covering her absence.
- Who will pay for the course – the nurse, the practice, the primary care trust?

Medico-legal issues

- Will need indemnity to practice – discuss with defence union.
- Consequences of failure to spot serious disease or unusual presentation.
- Nurses are responsible for own actions but liability may well be shared with the practice/trainer who will need to provide comprehensive training.
- Patients need to be aware they are not seeing a doctor as this may not be obvious.

Wider issues

- What is the job definition of the nurse practitioner?
- What is the validity of her "abbreviated" medical training?
- Need to develop clear job description and comprehensive protocols.
- Need to develop a restricted practice formulary for her use.
- Train receptionists on how to book patients to the nurse practitioner.
- Need to inform patients on using the service.
- Supervision of her consulting technique.

80. **"The NHS directly and indirectly discriminates against the elderly"**
Comment on:
- **direct age discrimination;**
- **redressing the balance using patient-centred care.**

INTRODUCTION

Standard one for the NSF for Older People is to target age discrimination which can be difficult to recognize as it can be direct or indirect.

ANSWER PLAN

Direct age discrimination
- Lack of accessibility of the health centre and other services.
- Attitudes – negative staff attitudes towards patients of high demand may influence delivery of care.
- Clinical failure e.g. actively underdetecting and treating depression.
- Failure to maximize preventative measures such as lifestyle suggestions.
- The elderly may well benefit most from many interventions which they may not be offered e.g. smoking cessation, warfarin therapy.
- Failure of services e.g. inadequate palliative care services in some areas.
- Minorities – racial and ethnic minority groups suffer even more discrimination in accessing services.
- Do Not Resuscitate decisions.
- Denial of interventions based on age alone is unacceptable.

Redressing the balance using patient-centred care
- Combat any communication difficulties.
- Provide evidence-based advice opportunistically and target high-risk groups.
- Develop and offer services e.g. incontinence clinics and recruit appropriately.
- Be aware of physical abuse of the elderly.
- Proactive system of review and recall.
- Use of polite, courteous behaviour.
- Aim to reduce social stagnation.
- Assess personal safety at home.
- Respect autonomy and privacy.
- Support carers.
- Dignity in terminal care.
- Provision of support in declining health.
- Personalized measures to identify all needs.
- Increase use of rehabilitative services.
- Regular audit to illustrate improvement.
- Appropriate funding targeted to areas of high need.

- Referral to secondary services regardless of age.
- Increase accessibility of primary care.

RELEVANT LITERATURE

National Service Framework (NSF) for Older People. *Dept of Health* 2001.

INTRODUCTION

The decision to prescribe is multifactorial. Evidence indicates that resistance to change is overcome by different types of cue in different doctors. This implies that individual styles require separate targeting and that traditional education cannot therefore be expected to bring about large scale change.

LIST

Intrinsic influences
- Assessment of clinical need.
- Importance of condition to be treated.
- Personal background and clinical experience with own patients in practice.
- Doctor's personality and keenness to try new treatments.
- Doctor's expectations of patients' likely compliance with medication.
- Doctor's perception of patients' expectations: one study showed if the GP felt the patient expected medication then they were ten times likelier to receive it. Patients who actually expected medication were only three times likelier to receive it.
- Willingness to prescribe without seeing patient.
- Knowledge and clear understanding of the actions and risk profile of a drug.
- Experience of using a drug yourself and forming a personal opinion of effectiveness and side-effects.
- Reinforcement of actions by positive feedback from patients.
- Inhibition of behaviour with negative reports and anecdotal evidence of adverse effects.
- Challenge from a specific event e.g. death of patient from amitriptyline overdose.
- Awareness of alternatives.
- Use of prescription to close difficult and time-consuming consultations.
- Accumulation of knowledge from continuous professional development e.g. articles, lectures (slow adaptive process).

Extrinsic influences
- Effect of the media on awareness and attitudes towards drugs.
- Patient pressure.
- Local and central pressures of cost.
- Practice policy/formulary.
- Opinions of trusted colleagues e.g. partner or local consultant.
- Direct exposure to new methods of practice e.g. appointment of recently-trained partner.

- Contact with other colleagues e.g. feedback from pharmacist regarding your prescriptions.
- Contact with and influence of pharmaceutical representatives.
- Evidence-based peer-reviewed journals.
- NICE guidance.
- PACT (Prescribing Analysis and Cost) data (?).

RELEVANT LITERATURE

A study of general practitioners' reasons for changing their prescribing behaviour. Armstrong, D et al., BMJ **312:** 949–952, 1996.

Factors which influence the decision whether or not to prescribe: the dilemma facing general practitioners. Bradley, C P BJGP **42:** 454–458, 1992.

Prescribing behaviour in clinical practice: patient's expectations and doctors' perceptions of patient expectations. Cockburn, J BMJ **315:** 520–523, 1997.

82. **Daisy Duke is a 79 year old lady who comes to see you smelling of alcohol and mentions her frequent falls. You are worried she will soon do herself some damage. How will you assess her risks and prevent further falls?**

INTRODUCTION

Falls are the largest cause of fatal accidents in the home and 80% of the victims are aged over 65. Every 5 hours an older person is killed by an accidental fall in the home.

About one-third of this age group fall at least once a year.

ANSWER PLAN

Identify risks

- Accurate history including past falls, use of alcohol.
- Detailed drug history and assess possible side effects e.g. sedation, confusion.
- Search for underlying medical condition e.g. visual impairment, vestibular disease, postural hypotension, hypoglycaemia.
- History from relatives and carers if possible.
- Appropriate clinical examination to find causes e.g. lying and standing BP.
- Lack of mobility and lack of muscle strength e.g. previous stroke.
- Psychological assessment – fear of falling also reduces amount of activity.
- Awareness of household hazards.
- General risk factors – age, female sex, previous falls.
- Is there a need for referral to a falls clinic?

Preventing falls and supporting evidence

Occupational therapy

- A home visit for hazard assessment and modification (e.g. poor lighting, need for rails, footwear) can reduce falls in and out of the home by a third.

Physiotherapy

- A programme of muscle strengthening and balance retraining e.g. Tai Chi, individually prescribed at home by a trained health professional is effective.

Medication review

- Withdrawal of psychotropic medication reduces falls but can be difficult to achieve.

Team approach
- Risk factor intervention programmes that take a multidisciplinary, multifactorial approach to health and the environment are effective in the elderly. An RCT of such an approach in nursing homes has shown a 19% reduction in falls.

Preventing damage from falls
- Osteoporosis treatments and hip protectors are effective and should be offered to high-risk patients.

General measures
- Primary care is well-placed to assess fears and worries.
- Personal emergency response systems can help confidence.
- Use of the media for increased awareness of the problem.
- Community strategies to provide information.

All this treatment works best when targeted toward high-risk individuals.

Resources implications for these interventions will be considerable but savings made may show cost-effectiveness in the future.

RELEVANT LITERATURE

Managing falls in older people. *DTB* **38(9):** 77–80, 2000.
Interventions for preventing falls in elderly people. *Cochrane Review* May 2001.
Guidelines for the prevention of falls in people over 65. Feder, G *et al.*, *BMJ* **321:** 1007–1011, 2000.

83. Jenny, your practice nurse, comes to you in distress and tells you she has just given an 8 week old baby the MMR vaccine instead of the DTP and Hib. What is your management of the situation?

INTRODUCTION

Behind most errors is a complex system of failure which needs to be identified and corrected, ideally in a no-blame culture.

FIVE POINT PLAN

Clinical issues
- Consider potential harm done.
- Check baby is well.
- Phone for help if needed e.g. public health or manufacturer.
- Probably no obvious increased risks in this situation.
- Need to still vaccinate with DTP.

Practice approach
- Involve all partners and practice manager.
- Nominate doctor to respond to parents.
- Continued support to parents in coming days.
- Critical incident investigation involves interviewing all parties.
- Try to establish causes in the systems of care involved.
- Institute immediate safety measures.
- Inform Primary Care Trust.
- PCT could help with press release or employ a media company if error goes public.
- May need to issue a statement accessible to all your patients.
- Requirement for disciplinary hearing for nurse.

Discussion with parents
- Expect an angry reaction.
- Clear space for a lengthy consultation.
- Be supportive and open to encourage venting and questions.
- Apologize. Acknowledge the error.
- Parents' opinions on safety of MMR.
- Could harm the doctor–patient relationship long-term.
- Arrange next contact perhaps by phone later that day.
- Inform about formal complaints procedure.

Effects on staff
- Important effect on nurse – needs support and guidance not punishment.
- Nurse has behaved with integrity.
- Stressful situation for the entire practice.
- Encourage staff to always admit mistakes.

- All staff will need to be supportive of the family.
- Hopefully a valuable learning experience.

Medico-legal/ethical issues
- Commenting to the press requires consent or is break of confidentiality.
- Involve defence union at early stage.
- Improve systems of practice to avoid errors in future.
- Raises issues of non-maleficence, beneficence and confidentiality.
- Keep comprehensive records.
- Danger of litigation.

84. What are the considerations in organizing an influenza vaccination programme in your practice?

INTRODUCTION

In the debilitated, influenza can kill. In pandemics, millions have died. Each year, it is the GP's responsibility to offer immunization to a defined high-risk population.

FIVE POINT PLAN

Practice matters
- Organize a practice meeting to discuss approach.
- Assess differences from previous year.
- Incorporate new national and local guidance.
- Consider buying power of local group and order sufficient vaccine.
- Develop clear, safe protocol for administration e.g. review of adverse reactions.
- Dedicated clinics, opportunistic, open-access or all the above?
- Booking arrangement e.g. by phone, on the Internet.
- Consider extra pressure on practice nurse.
- May reduce other available appointments.

Identify target group
- Use of computer to identify high-risk groups e.g. chronic heart disease, diabetes, age–sex register.
- Policy for contacting defaulters.
- Liaison with residential and nursing homes.

Promotion
- Personal invitation by letter or telephone.
- National and local publicity campaigns.
- Use of media e.g. articles for the local press or invite photographer.
- Posters in waiting room.

Teamwork approach
- Liaise with the district nurses to jab all those who are housebound or poorly mobile.
- Other specialist nurses e.g. diabetic or respiratory nurse can also help.
- Be ready to strike opportunistically in clinics.
- PCT is obliged to inform all over 65s about the vaccine and how to get it or help fund your attempts e.g. mail shot.

Research points
- Flu vaccine is only 50–70% effective in elderly patients and in those with depressed immune systems but mortality and costs of hospitalization are high.

- Basic organizational strategy can allow high vaccination rates.
- Designated clinics improve vaccination rates particularly in patients over 65 and those with cardiac disease.
- Uptake among patients < 65 can be improved by special information pamphlets.
- Offering at home improves uptake but is expensive.
- More than half of at-risk patients do not know they qualify for free flu vaccination.

INTRODUCTION

A clearly researched comparison of home versus hospital care would be useful. Unfortunately, an ethical randomized controlled trial would be a contradiction in terms.

ANSWER PLAN

Pros

- Expression of maternal preference is part of a healthy birth process.
- About 8% of women would prefer a home birth.
- Maternity services should be sensitive to the requirements of the local population.
- Care can be organized in GP obstetric units to best use local skills.
- New models of care may allow GP input to break through practice boundaries.
- Community midwives are increasingly keen on home delivery.
- Home deliveries are cheaper than in hospital.
- More continuity of care may produce a better birth experience.
- GPs retain a duty of care in an emergency and may have to attend unplanned delivery.

Evidence has shown

- Routine electronic monitoring during labour does not reduce perinatal mortality but does increase the chance of Caesarean section.
- Studies show that planned home births have a very low mortality rate (but data excludes higher risk births by definition).
- One study showed 65% of consultant obstetricians feel it is safe for low-risk pregnancies (but 35% felt it was less safe than hospital care).
- Low-risk pregnancies may have little or no benefit from obstetrician-led shared care compared to routine GP/midwife care.

Cons

- Doctors have become deskilled in this area and the vast majority do not wish to be involved in deliveries.
- GP registrars have little experience of normal delivery.
- Delivery rates are insufficient to maintain skills even if interested. This presents problems of ongoing training.
- Lack of personal round the clock availability of the modern GP.
- Difficulty of incorporating disruption to work responsibilities.
- The GP taking responsibility for delivery exempts himself from the Bolam test as it usually applies to GPs. He legally undertakes to provide a standard of care equivalent not to other GPs but to an obstetrician.
- Most practices are not equipped for home deliveries.
- Things go wrong very quickly.

Evidence has shown

- Despite a very low perinatal mortality rate, estimations suggest that 42% of deaths in healthy babies could be prevented by better care.
- Babies at high risk are safer under specialist hospital obstetric care (and a normal delivery is a retrospective diagnosis!).
- Only 75% of GPs currently providing intrapartum care want to continue.

RELEVANT LITERATURE

Changing Childbirth. *Dept of Health* 1993.
Should obstetricians see women with normal pregnancies? A multicentre RCT of routine antenatal care by general practitioners and midwives compared with shared care led by obstetricians. Tucker, J S *et al.*, *BMJ* **312:** 554–559, 1996.
Opinions of consultant obstetricians in the Northern region regarding the provision of intrapartum care by GPs. Frain, J P J *et al.*, *BJGP* **46:** 611–612, 1996.
Babies deaths linked to sub-optimal care. Dillner, L. *BMJ* **310:** 757, 1995.

INTRODUCTION

Cerebrovascular disease is the third most common cause of death in the developed world. The incidence is rising due to the elderly population. A GP will typically see four new strokes per year. Twenty-four per cent of the severely disabled are stroke victims.

FIVE POINT PLAN

Immediate management
- Attend promptly.
- Relevant medical examination and assessment of disability.
- Considerate liaison with family.
- Referral to hospital for CT within 48 hours or fast-track assessment clinic.

Rehabilitation services
- Stroke units are "gold-standard" being superior to other forms of stroke care. Benefits persist at 10 years.
- Early discharge, if disability allows, increases patient satisfaction and provides equivalent care provided they continue to be seen by a multi-disciplinary team.
- Greatest recovery occurs in the first 3 months and rehabilitation should be started as soon as the patient's condition permits.
- Outcome and disability is improved by use of occupational therapy e.g. access to disability aids, and physiotherapy.
- Speech and language therapy for dysphasics improves recovery.
- Agree long-term approach with patient, carers and family.

Therapeutics and stroke prevention
- Stroke victims have a 30% rate of recurrence in 5 years.
- *Facilitate lifestyle changes* especially smoking cessation (NNT =43).
- *Aspirin* – the International Stroke Trial (IST) and Chinese Acute Stroke Trial (CAST) involved 40 000 patients and showed that early aspirin improves rate of death and dependency in acute ischaemic stroke and reduces further serious vascular events by 25%.
- *Antihypertensives* – British Hypertension Society advises target of <140/85 mmHg.
- *Anticoagulation* – Consider for all stroke patients with atrial fibrillation to decrease recurrence by two-thirds.
- *Statins* can reduce further stroke by a quarter and the recent Heart Protection Study showed that 40 mg simvastatin can reduce incidence of a first stroke in high-risk patients regardless of cholesterol.
- *ACE inhibitors* – HOPE study showed that ACE inhibitor reduces primary and secondary risk of stroke in high-risk patients.

Social issues

- Availability of and support for the carer e.g. stroke association, respite care.
- Advice regarding driving.
- Prospects of going back to work.
- Emotional and social consequences may persist for many years e.g. anxiety over loss of role.
- Stroke patients feel neglected, frustrated and abandoned.

Long-term issues

- Post-discharge hospital review.
- Consider patient's changing needs and environment e.g. need for further information.
- Ongoing lifestyle review and control of risk factors.
- Look for symptoms of depression in patient and carers. Emotional distress is seen in 55% of caregivers.
- Awareness of financial aspects such as benefits.
- Practice organization e.g. need to identify those at risk, create registers and audit outcomes.

RELEVANT LITERATURE

National Clinical Guidelines for Stroke – Update. *The Intercollegiate Working Party for Stroke* (www.rcplondon.ac.uk) 2002.
Management of stroke. Govern, R *et al., Postgrad. Med. J.* **79:** 87–92, 2003.
Developing a primary care-based stroke service: a review of the qualitative literature. Murray, J *et al., BJGP* **53(2):** 137–142, 2003.
National Service Framework for Older People. *Dept of Health*, 2001.

87. A 45 year old lady whom you have treated in the past for depression confides that she is increasingly distressed by her 17 year old son coming in late and being loud and unruly. She asks if you would talk to him. What is your response?

INTRODUCTION

Patients who consult about someone else present a unique set of challenges but also deliver the opportunity for improving insight.

FIVE POINT PLAN

Issues for the mother
- Uncover her specific anxieties and worries about her son.
- Be aware of any further agenda.
- What is the social and family background?
- Is other support available?
- Increasing stress may lead to relapse of depression.

Doctor's agenda
- Awareness of the trust patient has in you but need to clarify her expectations.
- Need to be supportive and offer positive help.
- Evaluate how much of the problem lies within each party.
- Is this an appropriate role for a doctor? Are you looking for morbidity or being a family policeman?
- Balance possibility of providing genuine help with that of exacerbating problems and inviting personal danger.
- Could disrupt the doctor–patient relationship.
- May be time-consuming but further knowledge of the family dynamics may be very useful.

Issues regarding the son
- Is he your patient and is there mutual respect?
- Is he likely to appreciate or accept advice?
- Is there an underlying problem in need of help or is this just high spirits?
- Identify clear behavioural changes e.g. use of alcohol, possible violence.

Management options
- Problem of how to contact him in least threatening manner e.g. via mother, phone, letter or home visit.
- Problem of sensitively raising the issue.
- Consider offering to see mother and son together.
- Could compromise by raising issue when he next visits surgery if appropriate.

- Explain ethical problems and duty of confidentiality to all parties.

Follow-up
- Ongoing review and support for mother.
- Other agencies such as CPN, social worker, specific support groups may be of use.

88. List the potential advantages and disadvantages of telephone consultations. How would you structure such a consultation to avoid any problems?

INTRODUCTION

Use of the telephone in general practice is an increasingly important aspect of care. In some countries up to 25% of primary care contacts are by phone. Each must be seen as a true consultation rather than merely simple advice.

ANSWER PLAN

Advantages
- Vast majority of diagnoses are made on history alone.
- Convenient for patients.
- Rapid access for patients if well organized.
- Can be delegated to a suitable trained nurse and free the doctor for more complicated cases or other practice duties.
- Protocols are available to guide decisions as for NHS Direct.
- Proven value for monitoring chronic illness such as asthma.
- Evidence has shown that triage by telephone facilitates:
  - speedier access to medical services;
  - fewer home visits;
  - fewer extras in the surgery;
  - reduction in stress.

Disadvantages
- An essentially new consultation skill which requires further training.
- Loss of visual and behavioural clues (although that may change in the future!).
- Sub-optimal communication can lead to misunderstanding.
- Requires dedicated time to do properly.
- Patients need educating on calling protocols.
- Easy to bring pre-conceptions to the consultation.
- Lack of evidence of what skills are required.
- Need for quality control and audit.
- Needs guidance on good practice to avoid possible medicolegal problems.

The consultation
- Introduce self.
- Record details of patient, time etc.
- Gathering information:
  - gain patient's confidence;
  - systematic but positive, sympathetic approach;
  - careful relevant past history;
  - need to be in a position to make a reasonable clinical judgement;

- identify specific concerns.
- Consider likely diagnosis.
- Giving advice:
  - home management plan if appropriate;
  - assess caller's satisfaction with approach;
  - record-keeping contemporary with the consultation;
  - safety netting with explicit plan of when to call back.

RELEVANT LITERATURE

Telephone surgeries. Toon, P *Update* Aug. 2002.

INTRODUCTION

COPD is a chronic, slowly progressive disease characterized by airway obstruction and responsible for a great deal of morbidity and mortality. In over 90% of cases the sole cause is smoking. Doctors are guilty of focusing on acute exacerbations effectively rationing access to secondary care. COPD victims become disadvantaged, socially isolated and largely silent.

FIVE POINT PLAN

Issues for the patient
- Limitation of lifestyle.
- Loss of autonomy.
- Require motivation to stop smoking.
- Poor prognosis and high morbidity.

Issues for the doctor
- Awareness of current British Thoracic Society guidelines.
- Knowledge of local services.
- Self-awareness of own knowledge and experience in this area.
- Is referral for shared care needed?

Diagnostic issues
- A purely clinical diagnosis is decreasingly acceptable.
- Spirometry is the only method for early diagnosis in asymptomatic individuals. Compare this to the potentially misleading peak expiratory flow.
- Should be performed on all cases of suspected COPD.
- Comment on the reproducibility and specificity of FEV_1 as a diagnostic tool as well as a measure of the severity of disease.
- Subjective reporting of symptoms is still important.

Issues for the practice
- Population with high demand for medical services.
- Consider purchase of a spirometer.
- Would require appropriate training and regular calibration.
- Is there local availability of open-access spirometry?
- Consider screening mining population with spirometry.
- Development of practice guidelines.
- Influenza vaccination programme.
- Need for extra staff e.g. respiratory nurse.
- Computerized registers for cases and interventions.

Clinical management plan

- Health promotion including exercise and weight optimization.
- Smoking cessation is the only intervention which reduces rate of decline (potentially by half).
- Rational use of medications to alleviate symptoms e.g. β-agonists, anti-cholinergics, theophylline.
- Decide if or when to prescribe steroids e.g. after demonstrating reversibility on spirometry.
- Check inhaler technique.
- Practical aid to help patient cope with social limitations.
- Nurse-administered hospital-at-home care can be comparable to emergency admission in quality.
- Pulmonary rehabilitation has benefits at all stages of COPD for symptoms and social and psychological effects.
- It improves patients' exercise capacity, functional ability and quality of life, even though lung function does not change.

RELEVANT LITERATURE

The management of COPD. *MeReC Bulletin* **9(10):** 37–40, 1998.
BTS guidelines for the management of COPD. *Thorax* **52(suppl 5):** 1997.
Peak flow meters and spirometers in general practice. *DTB* **35(7):** 58–62, 1997.
Chronic obstructive pulmonary disease. *MeReC Briefing* **18:** 5–8, 2002.
Chronic obstructive pulmonary disease and primary care. Elkington, H *BJGP* **52(7):** 532–534, 2002.

INTRODUCTION

Few women ask for advice before conception despite the fact that the pre-birth environment can cause significant medical problems. One study of 143 females who became pregnant showed that 86% attended their GP in the previous 12 months and 46% for advice about contraception. Of 811 patients in 42 practices, less than 40% thought preconceptual counselling was essential and more than 10% thought it was a waste of time. Only 50% knew to take folic acid.

ANSWER PLAN

Diet and supplements
- Folic acid supplements: Low risk – 400 µg daily. High risk e.g. previous neural tube defect, diabetes, use of anticonvulsants – 5 mg daily, from before conception until week 12 of pregnancy. Some advocate population measures such as compulsory fortification of bread or flour.
- Iron – no need for routine iron supplement; measure haemoglobin if anaemia suspected. Women who are routinely given iron are more likely to have babies with low birth weight.
- Optimize weight with BMI between 19 and 26. Avoid slimming and aim for appropriate weight gain.
- Avoidance of excessive vitamin A e.g. liver products.
- For vegans, supplementation with iron and vitamins may be desirable.
- Vitamin D supplements for some ethnic groups e.g. Asian women who spend much time indoors and whose absorption of calcium may be impaired by an excess of wholemeal cereals.

Smoking
- Prevalence at booking is 16%. Smoking incurs increased risk of spontaneous abortion, preterm delivery, low birth weight and perinatal death.
- Many continue to smoke but interventions can have an effect.

Alcohol and drugs
- Minimize alcohol intake. Evidence suggests even low alcohol intake is associated with behaviour problems such as aggression and withdrawal detectable at age 7 years.
- Serious misuse of alcohol in pregnancy is widespread in most large urban areas.
- Fetal alcohol syndrome is the leading cause of learning disability.
- Withdrawal programme for alcohol and other drugs may require a specialist centre.

Genetic risk

- Those at increased risk of genetic disorders should have them fully explored before pregnancy.
- Specialized advice is essential at an early stage.

Occupational

- Work outside the home is not detrimental to fetal growth or pregnancy.
- Advice on risk avoidance in the workplace.
- Advice on statutory maternity pay.

RELEVANT LITERATURE

Preconception care: who needs it, who wants it and how should it be provided. Wallace, M et al., BJGP **48:** 963–966, 1998.

Folic acid and the prevention of neural tube defects (Editorial). Wald, N et al., BMJ **310:** 1019–1020, 1995.

Low level prenatal alcohol exposure was associated with adverse behavioural outcomes in children at 6 to 7 years of age. EBM **7:** 61, 2002.

Clinical Review – Pregnancy (part 1). Penn, Z GP March 2001.

91. Mr. Watson is a 75 year old patient whom you believe to be suffering from Parkinson's disease. Discuss the issues relating to his management.

INTRODUCTION

Ten thousand people are diagnosed with Parkinson's disease each year in the UK, and this figure is expected to rise as the number of elderly people in the general population increases.

FIVE POINT PLAN

Doctor issues
- How does the consultation make you feel?
- Need to ensure up to date with current best practice.
- Uncertainty of making a clinical diagnosis.

Communication issues
- Careful explanation of the disease, its implications etc.
- Is a lot of information at this stage in the patient's interests?
- Describe consulting skills required e.g. understand patient's perceptions and expectations.
- Principles of breaking bad news.

Early clinical management
- Progressive symptoms of tremor, rigidity and bradykinesia.
- Consider other causes of Parkinsonism.
- Drug management: use of L-Dopa, selegiline, dopamine agonists and COMT inhibitors and decision on when to start.
- Need for early referral for multi-disciplinary approach.

Chronic disease management
- Make a social assessment.
- Understand impact on life of patient, relatives and future carers.
- Medical management can be complex as symptoms progress.
- Nurse specialists help to preserve patient's sense of wellbeing with no increase in costs.
- Look for symptoms of anxiety and depression, which affect up to 50% and are underdiagnosed and undertreated.
- Look for and treat non-motor symptoms e.g. anxiety, depression, sexual dysfunction, pain.
- Surgical options in late disease may be of benefit.
- Use of patient support societies.

Wider issues
- Controversy over when to start L-Dopa treatment in the young.
- Recent data suggests ropinirole, a non-ergot dopamine agonist, may be neuroprotective.

- Uncertainty about best treatment remains and better trials are needed with end points of relevance.
- Heavy implication for resources due to growing population of elderly.
- Role of advance directives.

RELEVANT LITERATURE

Effects of community based nurses specialising in Parkinson's disease on health outcome and costs: randomised controlled trial. Jarman, B *et al., BMJ* **324:**1072, 2002.
National Service Framework for Older People. *Dept of Health* 2001.

92. A 75-year-old man presents whom you suspect to be suffering from chronic heart failure. You do not have a dedicated clinic for this. What will you aim to achieve on this first consultation and how will you co-ordinate his future care?

INTRODUCTION

Heart failure affects 8% of the over 65 year olds and its prevalence is increasing. It is inadequately managed but should be treated with the seriousness of a malignant disease. The median age of presentation is 76 years and most present to primary care. The aims of a first consultation need to be realistic.

FIVE-POINT PLAN

Patient issues
- What does he understand by "heart failure"?
- How is his life affected?
- Areas of particular concern and worry.
- Explore contributing risk factors.

Issues for the doctor
- Time management – a lot to get through in a complex consultation in limited time.
- Need to structure most important things first.
- Gain common understanding to help compliance with investigations and further treatment.
- Explain plan and correct misconceptions of the term "heart failure".
- Personal issues of keeping up to date with developments, awareness of practice or local protocols.

Diagnosis and treatment
- Clinical assessment e.g. symptoms, examination, search for causes, look for comorbidity e.g. hypertension.
- Advise on lifestyle changes e.g. dietary measures, smoking, exercise, salt.
- Risk assessment.
- Investigations – should have initial blood tests, 12-lead ECG and chest X-ray.
- Should also book echocardiogram if at all possible.
- Plan follow-up with results.
- Reasonable initial treatment may involve an ACE inhibitor and diuretic.
- Consider need for shared care with hospital specialist and future monitoring.

Issues for the primary care team
- Audit and development of local guidelines/protocols.
- Use of a computer register.
- Is open-access echo available?
- Need to reinforce lifestyle messages.
- Team approach with nominated doctor and nurse.
- Development of specialist clinic to review risk factors.
- Consider training of specialist nurse or health visitor.

Evidence base
- Many studies point to undertreatment of heart failure in the community.
- Nurse interventions have been shown to reduce readmissions for heart failure. Regular contact to review treatment and patient education are likely to contribute to this effect.
- ACE inhibitors should be used first line in ventricular dysfunction if not contraindicated. They have been shown to reduce mortality and hospitalization in heart failure with classic evidence.
  - **SOLVD** (1992) The Studies of Left Ventricular Dysfunction prevention trial treated 4228 patients with an ejection fraction less than 30% using enalapril. Over 3 years mortality was reduced by 8% with a 20% reduction in hospital admission.
  - **CONSENSUS** (1987) The Cooperative North Scandinavian Enalapril Survival Study showed a reduction in mortality of 40% at 6 months and 31% at 12 months in patients with severe CCF. Treating 1000 people with moderate CCF saved 16 lives and 116 hospital admissions.

RELEVANT LITERATURE

Diagnosis and treatment of heart failure due to left ventricular systolic dysfunction. *SIGN guideline No 35.*
Randomised controlled trial of specialist nurse intervention in heart failure. Blue, L et al., *BMJ* **323:** 715–718, 2001.
Management of chronic heart failure. Cowie, M R et al., *BMJ* **325:** 422–425, 2002.

INTRODUCTION

Domestic violence is the term used to describe a type of physical, emotional, sexual and psychological abuse. As many as one in four women suffer violence at the hands of men with whom they share an intimate relationship. It crosses all social and ethnic boundaries.

FIVE POINT PLAN

Patient issues
- Use of a "calling card" hiding the real agenda.
- Sense of helplessness and low self-esteem leading to psychiatric morbidity.
- Fears of stigma and socioeconomic isolation.
- Without intervention, problem usually escalates.

Index of suspicion
- Consider diagnosis based on clues in the consultation.
- Clues include unexplained injuries, inconsistencies, evasive manner, clues in the notes, persistent presentation with minor illness, history of attempted suicide, depression.
- Anxiety is more strongly associated with domestic violence than depression.

Doctor issues
- Doctor's lack of confidence in ability to help.
- Moral obligation at least to act as a signpost to local services.
- Emphasize confidentiality.
- Ask! Doctors rarely do. Be sensitive and non-threatening. Evidence shows that those affected want to be asked directly and those not affected do not mind being asked.
- Assess present situation gathering information about sources of support, living circumstances etc.
- Clear documentation including verbatim history, times and dates, description of injuries (consider photographs).
- Danger of becoming involved as witness.
- Assess for signs of depression.

Care of children
- Mother may fear disturbance of relationship with father.
- Are children in danger?
- Consider referral to social services if at risk. Try to get patient's consent but you must act in their best interests. Further advice may be useful.

Advise and plan

- Explanation that domestic violence is illegal and that the patient is a victim.
- Explain physical and emotional consequences of ongoing abuse.
- Provide written information on legal options and obtaining help from police domestic violence units, Womens' Aid National Helpline, local authority social service and housing departments. Offer help in contacting them.
- Empower patient's decision by encouraging autonomy and self-determination.
- Be available to discuss again.
- Unfortunately there is a lack of evidence as to effectiveness of interventions.

RELEVANT LITERATURE

Domestic violence in families with children: Guidance for primary health care professionals. Shakespeare, J *RCGP* 2002 (www.rcgp.org.uk).
Reported frequency of domestic violence: cross sectional survey of women attending general practice. Bradley, F *et al.*, *BMJ* **324:** 271, 2002.

94. Linda is a 22 year old patient of yours with schizophrenia who has recently been discharged from hospital. She has a history of self-harm and lives with her mother. She tells you that she and her boyfriend are intending to have a child. What areas should be considered in her ongoing care?

INTRODUCTION

Schizophrenia affects one person in a hundred at some stage in life. Frequently, incomplete recovery and further relapses are the rule.

FIVE POINT PLAN

Issues related to pregnancy
- Is this a sign of impending crisis? Is she already pregnant?
- Explore reasons for wanting children.
- Need for psychosexual help.
- Ability to function as parent may be impaired.
- Specific preconceptual advice e.g. folate, stop alcohol.
- Specialist advice will be needed.
- Issues of drug treatment through pregnancy require specialist advice.
- Need for explanation of risks following childbirth.
- Risk of offspring suffering from schizophrenia rises to 40% if both parents are sufferers.

Multidisciplinary care
- Shared care with all members of the team of hospital consultant, GP, key worker e.g. community psychiatric nurse.
- Assessment of required level of supervision and a clear individual care plan.
- Agreed local policies on GP versus hospital responsibilities e.g. criteria for admission.
- Awareness of Mental Health Act.
- NICE requires case registers and regular checks on health.

Family issues
- Strong support for mother will be needed through pregnancy.
- High levels of criticism, hostility and over-involvement make patients up to four times more likely to relapse.
- Assess needs of other family members and need for family intervention programme.

Treatment and maintenance
- Should have a prepared plan for early treatment and crisis intervention.
- Opportunistically look for signs of stress, tension, relapse or depression.
- Medical monitoring of drug levels.

- Measures to minimize the risk of losing contact.
- Facilitate ongoing education and support for patients.

Social issues
- Ongoing assessment of issues of daily living and driving restrictions.
- Availability of allowances e.g. disability benefit.
- Encouragement to maintain function, work and fulfil useful role.
- Availability of voluntary agencies e.g. SANE, MIND.

RELEVANT LITERATURE

Schizophrenia: core interventions in the treatment and management of schizophrenia in primary and secondary care. *NICE* Dec 2002.

95. **The practice manager receives a complaint from a 33 year old female that one of the partners in the practice made her feel "uncomfortable" while being examined undressed. The practice manager says she does not want to take it further but feels she should mention it. She brings this up at a practice meeting asking for a response from the five partners. What issues does this raise?**

INTRODUCTION

In a culture of complaint, practices may have to deal with a number of allegations.

FIVE POINT PLAN

Doctors' reaction
- Awareness of personal feelings as to the nature of the information.
- Hope that it is just a misunderstanding but need to take it seriously.
- Awareness of own knowledge of partner and personal relationship with same.
- Non-judgemental support for colleague.
- A very tricky situation which strikes at the core of the practice.
- Personal feelings on blowing the whistle.
- Does it affects your feelings towards your colleague even if innocent?

Information gathering
- Get the view of the accused – obtain partner's experiences with this patient.
- What was the nature of the examination?
- Urgent need to discuss this with the patient.
- Assess patient's intent to proceed with complaint.

Patient interview
- Consider interview by different doctor.
- Consider presence of nurse as chaperone and witness.
- Sensitive non-judgemental approach needed.
- Gather clear, accurate history of events.
- Gather all information to gauge whether just a breakdown in communication in this doctor–patient relationship.
- Assess motives.
- Reassure that the situation will be looked into and that there is no need to see this doctor again and plan next contact.
- Treat presenting complaint appropriately.

Practice aspects
- Appropriate complaints procedure in place – does this letter constitute a formal complaint?

- Need to act urgently on serious implication of sexual assault while being aware of possible false accusation.
- Rumours may reflect on the practice even if not substantiated.
- Press may become involved and you would be invited to comment. If so ensure confidentiality.
- Concern over future relationship with this patient.
- Discuss with defence union/PCT/GMC.
- Formulate plan to respond promptly.

Chaperone policy
- Decision to use chaperone for future consultations/examinations with this patient.
- Concern over availability of chaperones – may need to offer new appointment.
- Evidence suggests that most women wish to be offered chaperones for intimate examination and see it as a sign of respect.
- Although guidelines do exist this is currently seen more as an area for excellent communication and shared-decision making rather than rigid policy. Verbal permission should be obtained.
- Keep notes of decisions made.

RELEVANT LITERATURE

Attitudes of patients towards the use of chaperones in primary care. Whitford, D L et al., *BJGP* **51(5):** 381–383, 2001.

Discuss the following aspects of the treatment of depression in general practice with reference to the evidence in these areas.
- **Diagnostic difficulties.**
- **Therapeutic approaches.**

INTRODUCTION

Depression is a widespread and commonly overlooked diagnosis. Primary care physicians are ideally placed to find and treat it. The 1992 Defeat Depression Campaign (RCGP consensus statement) advocated checklists for depression, education of GPs, longer consultations and use of questionnaires.

ANSWER PLAN

Diagnostic difficulties
- Doctors overlook 30–50% of depression.
- Diagnosis requires high index of suspicion and a need to search for possible underlying physical illness.
- Better consultation skills such as the use of open questioning and the need for longer consultations improve likelihood of recognizing depression.
- However, education should also increase detection but The Hampshire Depression Project RCT in 60 practices, although well received, showed no improvement in recognition of depression or patient outcome.
- Screening tools such as the two-question test may increase detection. They tend to be fairly sensitive but not very specific (too many false positives).
- Important to screen for alcohol e.g. CAGE questionnaire.
- Use depression scale to aid follow-up.
- Depressive symptoms are distributed continuously in the population and can change quickly. This makes diagnosis tricky.
- Any cut off in the level or duration of symptoms is felt by some GPs to be fairly arbitrary. Each practitioner's threshold for treatment is different.

Therapeutic approaches

Drugs
- All antidepressants are equally effective. Generally SSRIs tend to be prescribed over tricyclics due to being better tolerated.
- None has been shown to work any quicker than any other and all have side effects.
- Drugs are effective in only 50–60% and the delay to onset is a major stumbling block to compliance.
- Switching therapies causes further delay and many suffer side effects.

- Many practitioners doubt the effectiveness of antidepressants in the face of social problems despite guidelines which recommend treatment regardless of cause.
- Patients are often reluctant to accept drugs. Most of the British public thinks that depression is due to adverse life events and that counselling should be offered. This worsens compliance.

Intervention by counsellors
- RCTs have shown different standardized approaches to counselling (such as cognitive-behavioural and problem-solving) have equivalent efficacy to drugs in treating major depression. They used specially trained counsellors who adhered to a protocol.
- In one study unstandardized generic counselling was as effective at 12 months as antidepressant treatment for mild to moderate depression although patients receiving antidepressants may recover more quickly. They concluded GPs should allow patients to choose.
- No study has directly compared specific versus generic counselling as yet.

RELEVANT LITERATURE

Recognition and management of depression in general practice: consensus statement. Paykel, E S *BMJ* **305:** 198–202, 1992.

Specific issues in depression *MeReC Briefing No 17* April 2002.

Effects of a clinical practice guideline and practice-based education on detection and outcome of depression in primary care: Hampshire depression project randomised controlled trial. Thompson, C *et al., Lancet* **355:** 185–191, 2000.

Should general practitioners refer patients with major depression to counsellors? A review of current published evidence. Churchill, R *et al., BJGP* **49(9):** 738–743, 1999.

Why can't GPs follow guidelines on depression? Kendrick, T *BMJ* **320:** 200–201, 2000.

Antidepressant drugs and generic counselling for treatment of major depression in primary care: randomised trial with patient preference arms. Chilvers, C *et al., BMJ* **322:** 772, 2001.

Managing depression in primary care. Wagner, E *et al., BMJ* **322:** 746–747, 2001.

INTRODUCTION

Insomnia is a common symptom with four out of ten people complaining they often sleep poorly. Benzodiazepine prescription has declined substantially in recent years but large numbers are still prescribed for anxiety, insomnia and drug misusers. One aspect of standard 3 of the NSF for Mental Health is the need for responsible prescribing and audit of these drugs.

FIVE POINT PLAN

Patient Issues
- Are the underlying reasons for presentation sound?
- Associated social circumstances and problems e.g. stress, bereavement.
- Understanding of short and long-term effects e.g. potential dependence.
- Use of alcohol – was diazepam for alcohol withdrawal?
- Use of any other drugs either recreationally or for symptoms.

Doctor issues
- The need for good communication skills and a non-judgemental approach.
- Self-awareness e.g. irritation at colleague if lack of substantial symptoms, perceived pressure to prescribe.
- Reassess diagnosis – is there underlying physical or mental illness?
- Is your colleague available or is patient shopping around?
- Prior impression of partner's practices.
- Concern over alienating partner if challenged.

Practice issues
- Why were such large doses used?
- Issues of competence regarding colleague will reflect on practice.
- Prescribing policy for hypnotics and the need for a practice formulary.
- Structured programme for identifying benzodiazepine users.

Treatment issues
- Pros and cons of continuing drug management e.g. by reducing dose.
- Availability of further help e.g. relaxation guides, behavioural and cognitive therapy.
- Advice on "sleep hygiene".
- Education on side effects e.g. effect on driving and increased falls in elderly.
- Need for review and follow-up with same doctor each time.

Wider issues

- Maleficence: benzodiazepines and the potential for addiction.
- Committee on the Safety of Medicines only recommends treatment with benzodiazepines for insomnia if severe and disabling and if possible only intermittently.
- New standards of clinical governance require audits of prescribing rates, diagnoses and record-keeping of such drugs.

RELEVANT LITERATURE

National Service Framework (NSF) Digest for Mental Health. Dept of Health.
An update on benzodiazepine and non-benzodiazepine hypnotics. *MeReC Briefing No 17,* April 2002.

98. Mrs. Jones is 51 years old. She tells you her mother who suffered from angina died 2 years ago following a fractured femur and asks you to prescribe hormone replacement therapy. How would you manage this consultation?

INTRODUCTION

This is a complex consultation not least because of rapidly developing research regarding the use of HRT. Is she worried about her heart, her bones, menopausal symptoms or is she grieving?

FIVE POINT PLAN

Issues for the patient
- Explore patient's specific concerns – what is her true agenda?
- Is there an element of bereavement?
- Social circumstances e.g. marriage and children at home.
- Explore patient's understanding of effects of HRT.
- Does she also have menopausal symptoms?

Issues for the doctor
- Take time – advice may well be your treatment for this consultation.
- Develop a rapport that allows you to get to the core of her concerns.
- Opportunity to advise on lifestyle changes that can have an effect e.g. physical activity, smoking.
- Retrospectively assesses and discuss mother's risk factors for osteoporosis such as age, use of steroids.
- Evaluate patient's personal risk profile for osteoporosis. The Royal College of Physicians has guidelines which include family history of osteoporosis.
- Important to be aware of current evidence in a rapidly changing field.

Sharing decision-making
- Patient does not need treatment today so take time with explanation and discuss options.
- Prescription depends on current evidence and personal risks/attitudes.
- Explanation of physiology and risk-benefit assessment.
- Genuine mutual concern over osteoporosis should lead to bone density screening (preferably dual X-ray absorptiometry) before initiating treatment.
- Discussion of therapeutic alternatives and different options (for menopausal symptoms or future osteoporosis or IHD).
- Given written information.
- Plan review to rediscuss.
- Record patient's choice in notes.

Issues for the practice
- Role of clinical nurse for education and monitoring lifestyle risk factors.
- Availability of written material, videos etc.
- Practice formulary for prescribing.
- Identifying high-risk cases and use of densitometry.

Use of HRT
- **Menopausal symptoms.** For many the benefits of short-term (2–3 years) relief of symptoms outweigh any small increased risks.
- **Cardiac.** HRT is of no current value in preventing cardiac events.
- **Osteoporosis.** There is a clear benefit for patients with proven osteoporosis and those at high risk. It can almost halve the risk of osteoporotic fracture if given for 5–10 years but benefit is quickly lost on stopping. Likely to be more cost-effective when older e.g. >65 years but controversy persists on when best to start. Use depends on personal history, risk factors and preference and should be weighed against a small increase in breast malignancy, DVT and stroke.

RELEVANT LITERATURE

Safety Update on Long-term HRT. *Current Problems in Pharmacovigilance.* MCA Oct 2002.
Making decisions about hormone replacement therapy. Rymer, J *et al., BMJ* **326:** 322–326, 2003.

99. One of your partners continually turns up late for his surgeries. He refuses to see extra patients at the end of surgery and you are increasingly having to cover for him. You arrange a meeting with the rest of the partners. What will you wish to discuss?

INTRODUCTION

Irregularity of a colleague's behaviour may indicate an underlying cause and could have far-reaching consequences for patient care and service delivery.

FIVE POINT PLAN

Approaching the partner
- Recognize difficulty of combining business and personal relationship.
- Diplomatic technique, perhaps nominating least threatening doctor.
- Understand and acknowledge partner's point of view.
- Assess underlying reasons sympathetically e.g. family or work problems
- Signs of burnout?
- Has he or she contacted further help e.g. own GP?
- Use of alcohol.

Problems for the partnership
- Additional burden on other staff.
- Concern over his current fitness to practise.
- Concerns for the future of the practice.
- The need to maintain supportive relationship between all partners.
- Requirement for ongoing clinical governance.
- Context of any previous problems.

Practice organization
- Ensure ongoing provision of routine and emergency care.
- May require temporary leave of the partner.
- May need a locum.
- Need for good communication strategy for staff and patients.
- Are there underlying problems within the practice which should be reorganized?
- Adequacy of complaints procedures.

Medico-legal and ethical issues
- Duty of confidentiality.
- Patients may have instituted complaints proceedings already.
- Duty of care and the need to protect patients.

Future plan
- Try and agree plan for the future e.g. time off, stress-management.
- Reassess regularly.

- Make contingency plans to cover workload.
- Consider need to involve other agencies e.g. National Counselling Service for sick doctors, BMA's hotline for distressed doctors, GMC.
- Be supportive.

RELEVANT LITERATURE

Good Medical Practice. *General Medical Council* 1998.

INTRODUCTION

The National Asthma Campaign estimates that one in three adults and one in eight children have current symptomatic asthma with over 5 million people receiving treatment. Most patients with long-term asthma are managed in general practice.

FIVE POINT PLAN

Define aims
- Discussion with partners to agree aims and organizational aspects.
- Aims of treatment are to control symptoms, prevent exacerbations, optimize pulmonary function and minimize side effects.

Define methods
- Review current guidelines from British Thoracic Society (2003).
- Consider needs of entire practice population.
- Case identification of asthmatics – opportunistically or identification using records.
- Maintain practice-based register of all asthmatics.
- Select parameters of assessment e.g. use of inhalers.
- Create protocols for intervention.

Practice organization
- Trained practice nurses are highly effective for regular review of patients.
- Assess implications for other services e.g. fewer appointments.
- Is appropriate equipment available e.g. for testing inhaler technique?
- Ensure affected patients are aware of any changes.

Evidence-based approach and the use of guidelines
- Apply BTS guidelines with a stepwise approach to care.
- Familiarize with newer drugs such as leukotriene receptor antagonists and long-acting β2 agonists.
- Customized asthma action plans have been shown to improve control, decrease absence from work/school and reduce need for consultations.
- Regular structured clinic review improves outcomes.
- Titrate medication according to symptoms.
- Inhaler devices tested for technique and chosen to suit individual patient.
- Prescribe a peak flow meter. Be aware that over-reading from peak-flow meters may cause undertreatment.

- Healthcare professionals underestimate symptoms so use the Royal College of Physicians' three simple questions at every asthma consultation:
  - have you had difficulty sleeping due to asthma symptoms?
  - have you had your usual asthma symptoms during the day?
  - has asthma interfered with your usual activities?

Follow-up and audit
- Meet with partners to discuss findings of audit.
- Audit data on changes in chosen parameters.
- Revise protocol as needed.

RELEVANT LITERATURE

British guidelines on the management of asthma. *BTS/SIGN* 2003.

INTRODUCTION

UTI affects 3–5% of girls and 1–2% of boys during childhood. Practical difficulties with collecting urine mean the diagnosis is easily missed in the young. The long-term consequences include chronic renal failure and dialysis. Guidelines exist to aid the GP.

FIVE POINT PLAN

Issues for the doctor
- Awareness of guidelines.
- Careful assessment and consideration of diagnosis.
- Practical difficulties of dealing with a febrile child.

Issues for the practice
- Agreed methods for organization of urine collection.
- Awareness of all staff regarding collection of samples.
- Use of microscopy within the practice.
- Preparation of written advice for parents.
- Liaison with local paediatrician.
- Protocols for direct access to ultrasound/DMSA scan.

Clinical management
- Need to prove diagnosis – use of microscopy, urinalysis, MSU for culture and sensitivity.
- Antibiotic protocol for immediate management.
- Referral for investigation to detect underlying cause.

Follow-up
- Consider need for future prophylactic antibiotics after first or subsequent UTI.
- Need for post-treatment sample.
- Shared-care model.

Related evidence
- Royal College of Physicians guidelines (1991) state any infant with fever >38.5°C with no obvious source requires fresh MSU sample to be taken.
- In a 1997 study, 74% of GPs were unaware of the 1991 guidelines.
- *E. coli* accounts for about three quarters of all pathogens.
- Seven to 10 days of antibiotics are better than shorter courses.
- Long-term antibiotic therapy does prevent further infections.
- Obstructive anomalies are found in up to 4% and vesicoureteric reflux in up to 40% of children being investigated for their first UTI.

- The incidence of new renal scars rises with each episode of infection.
- Very low risk of renal damage if UTI occurs after fourth birthday.
- Simple measures acceptable to parents reduce the chance of a contaminated sample.
- Children with proven UTI have had more consultations for febrile illness than controls suggesting previous missed diagnoses.

RELEVANT LITERATURE

The management of urinary tract infection in children. *DTB* **35(9):** 72, 1997.
Home collection of urine for culture from infants by three methods: survey of parents' preferences and bacterial contamination rates. Liaw, L C T *et al., BMJ* **320:** 1312–1313, 2000.
Urinary tract infection in children. Larcombe, J *BMJ* **319:** 1173–1175,1999.

INTRODUCTION

Alcohol causes 28 000 premature deaths per year. Six per cent of men drink more than 50 units per week. Related costs to the NHS may reach £400 million pounds per year.

ANSWER PLAN

GPs can be alerted to the presence of problem drinking in several ways.

Clinical presentations
- Physical symptoms – any system of the body can be affected e.g. gastritis, neuropathy, unexplained fractures.
- Psychological symptoms – e.g. anxiety, depression, mood fluctuations, sexual problems.
- Comorbidity with substance abuse.
- Features of dependence e.g. smelling of alcohol, sweating, tremor, agitation.
- Complications following accidents or violence.

Social presentations
- Absenteeism and request for sick notes.
- Occupation e.g. publican, businessmen with long absences from family.
- Third-party presentation of family members e.g. due to marital conflict.
- Emotional and behavioural problems in the children.
- Child abuse.
- Awareness of domestic violence.

Screening
- Simple opportunistic enquiry regarding lifestyles e.g. at new patient registration.
- Simple screening tools such as the **CAGE** questionnaire:
  - ever felt you should **C**ut down on your drinking?
  - have people **A**nnoyed you by criticizing your drinking?
  - have you ever felt **G**uilty about your drinking?
  - have you ever had an **E**ye-opener?
- **AUDIT Questionnaire** (Alcohol Use Disorder Identification Test) is a suitable tool for more severe drinkers in primary care
- **Laboratory tests** e.g. raised GGT, raised MCV, altered LFTs (indicative rather than diagnostic)

Relevant evidence

- Well-planned brief interventions include advice with a leaflet, self-help manual, feedback of blood tests or feedback on how patient's drinking compares with the population.
- They can help well-motivated people cut down typically by 25%.
- 70% of eligible drinkers decline to take part in such studies.
- Brief intervention by a non-specialist can be as effective as longer specialist interventions and reduction can be sustained at 48 months.
- Primary prevention in 8–25 year group not shown in randomized controlled trials to be particularly effective.
- Intervention is cheap and cost-effective but not widely adopted.
- GPs have shown reluctance to treat alcohol problems or attend training in the area due partly to pessimism at the outcome and other pressures of work.

RELEVANT LITERATURE

Managing the heavy drinker in primary care. *DTB* **38**(8): 68–72, Aug 2000.
Effectiveness of general practice intervention for patients with harmful alcohol consumption. Anderson, P *BJGP* **43**: 386–389,1993.

103. How do you manage the case of a 16 year old girl who tells you her acne is getting worse despite your treatment?

INTRODUCTION

Acne is a treatable condition with a complex aetiology that commonly presents to the GP. It affects four in five 16 year old girls and 85% of boys. Its potential for cutaneous and emotional scarring mean it is not a minor disease.

FIVE POINT PLAN

Patient factors
- What are her expectations of you, her understanding and worries?
- May be stigmatized by even minor acne.
- Consider impact on life e.g. effect on participation in sport, socializing, choice of clothing?
- False beliefs – may blame herself or feel it is a result of poor hygiene.
- May have self treated with other preparations.
- Compliance issues.
- Contraceptive requirements.

Doctor's approach
- Be aware of psychological impact and use holistic approach.
- Dispel misconceptions e.g. that acne is caused by lack of hygiene (blackheads are oxidized sebum not dirt) or eating chocolate (dietary changes have little impact).
- Educational approach facilitates realistic outcomes e.g. general advice on use of cosmetics, length of treatment needed.
- Determine severity i.e. presence of comedones, pustules, nodules and scarring.
- Diagnostic issues e.g. accuracy of clinical diagnosis.
- Assess why treatment has apparently failed e.g. how long has she been on treatment? There may be little improvement in the first month.

Therapeutics
- Need to start effective treatment early to prevent scarring.
- Use of topical retinoids – adapalene, tretinoin, isotretinoin.
- Topical antibiotics with benzoyl peroxide are superior to topical antibiotics alone and help avoid antibiotic resistance.
- Use of antiandrogens (cyproterone/oestrogen combination) if also requiring contraception.
- Need for specialist referral. Oral isotretinoin is highly effective but only available in secondary care as highly teratogenic. Speed access by doing initial blood tests e.g. lipids, LFTs.
- Follow up to monitor resistance to treatment and review drugs regime regularly.

Developing a practice policy
- Lack of UK guidelines.
- Evidence is weak for benefits of different approaches creating uncertainty.
- Develop practice consistency with guidelines and referral policy.
- Role of practice nurse e.g. when advising on contraception.
- Consider role of local pharmacist in first-line treatment.
- Use of written material.

Wider issues
- Prescribing of oral isotretinoin in primary care: financial implications versus potential to reduce waiting times for secondary care.
- Further research into evidence base is in progress.

RELEVANT LITERATURE

Acne Vulgaris. Webster, G. *BMJ* **325:** *475-479*, 2002.
Referral Advice. A guide to appropriate referral from general to specialist services. London, NICE, 2001.

INTRODUCTION

Such requests have not been a central element of a GP's job in the past but are likely to become more frequent as time goes on. The consequences of such requests can be serious.

FIVE POINT PLAN

Father's agenda
- What specifically triggered the request?
- Assess his underlying motives.
- Understanding of the consequences of the request.
- Are there signs of underlying deeper anxiety or depression?

Family issues
- Are marital difficulties cause or effect?
- Discussion with wife would be desirable.
- Result could provoke despair and desperation and risk ending the marriage.
- Potential of the test to harm child's social and financial support.
- Are there other children or family members whose life will be affected?
- Need to seek legal advice.

Doctor's position
- Consider personal safety in volatile situation.
- Experience or uncertainty of dealing with such a request.
- Is this really your job? Recognize feelings e.g. potential irritation that you are neither a marriage counsellor nor a solicitor.
- Recognize personal moral code regarding paternity testing.
- Influence of background knowledge of family dynamics and social circumstances.
- Would it be better to discuss with wife and return if necessary?
- Use of communication skills to facilitate balanced decision on whether to proceed.
- Knowledge of the practicalities of testing.
- Is some sort of counselling a suitable approach?
- Advice to seek legal opinion from solicitor.
- Ensure good record keeping.

Ethical/legal issues
- Risk that facilitating the test may destabilize family and expose you to serious criticism.
- BMA advice is not to test children if it is not in the child's best interests.

- Children's Act requires doctors to act in the best interests of the child.
- Issues of consent – usually only required from one parent with parental responsibility.
- Consequences of availability of paternity tests on the Internet.
- Increasing availability of genetic tests will cause further dilemmas.

Wider issues
- Lack of availability of paternity tests on the NHS.
- Is there a need for a practice protocol for such requests?
- Long-term effects on society of such testing e.g. increasing number of one-parent families.

RELEVANT LITERATURE

The Children Act 1989. www.hmso.gov.uk

INTRODUCTION

With the advent of modern drugs and an increased culture of openness, erectile dysfunction has become an increasingly common diagnosis.

FIVE POINT PLAN

Patient factors
- Embarrassment and effects on self-esteem.
- Fear of lack of confidentiality.
- What are his expectations of the consult?
- Need for openness with partner.
- Is he sufficiently motivated for non-drug types of therapy?

Doctor issues
- Reassure patient of privacy.
- Concern over pressure of time.
- Lack of training in sexual health.
- Awareness of local protocols and routes for referral.
- Sensitive but directed consultation skills will reduce mutual embarrassment.
- Is there a need to assess with partner?
- Detailed history including medications, relationship history, sexual history.
- Exclude psychiatric problem which may be primary or as a complication, e.g. anxiety, depression, alcoholism.
- Examination may be limited to blood pressure, examination of external genitalia and as indicated by history.
- Exclude underlying medical problems, e.g. glucose test for diabetes.
- Establish treatment goals and arrange follow up.

Therapeutics
- General lifestyle advice e.g. stop smoking, exercise, reduce alcohol, relaxation.
- Discuss different treatment options e.g. use of oral sildenafil or sublingual apomorphine, alprostadil by intracavernosal injection or transurethral application
- Is NHS psychosexual counselling available locally?
- Informed consent for choice of treatment or referral.
- Contact with self-help groups such as The Impotence Association.

Primary care team
- Possible delegation to specialist nurses working within protocols.
- Potential role for GP with special interest.
- Use of shared-care guidelines with clear referral policy to a secondary multidisciplinary team.

Broader issues

- Patients obtaining Viagra elsewhere e.g. Internet.
- Availability of pharmacological agents or vacuum devices on the NHS.
- Ethics of rationing drugs on the NHS.
- Cost implications to the NHS of even newer drugs.

RELEVANT LITERATURE

UK management guidelines for erectile dysfunction. Ralph, D. *et al. BMJ* **321:** 499-503, 2000.
Management of male sexual problems. Wylie, K. *Doctor Update*, Feb. 2003.

THE 4 MINUTE VIVAS

The emphasis of the oral part of the MRCGP is aimed at these three broad areas:

- Communication;
- Professional values;
- Personal and professional growth.

Communication encompasses verbal and non-verbal communication techniques, skills for effective information transfer and principles of communication and consultation models.

Professional values are moral and ethical issues, patient autonomy, medico-legal issues, flexibility and tolerance, implications of styles of practice, roles of health professionals and cultural and social factors.

Personal and professional growth focuses on continuing professional development, self-appraisal and evaluation, stress-awareness and management, burnout and change management.

These are tested in four contexts:

- Care of the patient;
- Working with colleagues ;
- The social role of general practice;
- Personal responsibilities for care, decisions and outcomes.

The oral comprises two similarly-structured 20-minute sessions each with a pair of examiners. An observer may also be present. The sessions are separated by a 5 minute break for changing tables. The examiners will have no knowledge of your performance in the other modules of the exam or the other viva. They will have planned your orals in advance so as to ensure examination of different topics and they will take it in turns to question you. They will typically cover five questions per table. The watch on the desk counts 4 minutes per question. One speaks while the other marks.

The orals exist to test areas not tested in the other modules. They will assess your decision-making processes in day-to-day practice and ability to justify your conclusions in the face of critical challenge from the examiners. It is important to demonstrate this process in your dialogue. The journey is often more highly weighted in the marking scheme than the destination.

The questions can cover any area of practice and clinical scenarios are often used to illustrate not particular clinical solutions but your approach to them e.g. use of consultation skills. It is sometimes useful to remember the same approach you have used in the written paper. This adds value to the idea of doing the viva module in the same sitting of the exam as the written paper. You must know what is in current journals in particular the *BMJ* and *BJGP* and in the media generally. A broad preparation for the written paper will ensure you stumble across most of the topics and issues that are current. Consider your position in advance on these issues and practice presenting them in a concise, well-structured and confident manner.

Listening carefully to the question will help you realize what areas and contexts are being tested and allow you to target the structure of your answer.

Practice of the technique is essential because it is surprisingly difficult to give good viva answers even on subjects with which you are familiar. Because it can be difficult for many to get good practice, I have included a series of sample questions to try. The first group of questions are supplemented by notes which highlight important points. Additional questions are included to allow further practice.

As classical dilemmas frequently appear in both the written and oral parts of the MRCGP, a further list of these is included for you to consider.

The viva questions are best practised in a semi-formal environment with a friend or colleague asking the questions. This enables interactivity and is more realistic allowing the questioner to go off at a tangent. It also permits the process of challenging your opinions. If you have a strong opinion do not be afraid to express it but it will need balance to show you have considered the other options. As long as you can justify your thoughts the examiners will appreciate a bit of enthusiasm and it may well benefit you. Remember to refer to evidence in your answers if it seems relevant.

Difficulty will increase as you are challenged and you may reach a point beyond which you cannot go. It will feel uncomfortable but do not be put off. It is all part of assessing your limits.

Typically, the initial question may set the scene before the follow-up questions focus on the area the examiners are testing. I have therefore presented the sample questions in the following format:

STEM QUESTION
- FOLLOW-UP QUESTION
- FOLLOW-UP QUESTION

The pace is rapid. Say your piece and then stop. The examiners will be ready with their follow-up.

PRACTICE VIVAS WITH NOTES

VIVA TABLE 1

Question 1
- What might be the value of patient-held records?
- What would be the advantages for patients?
- How might it work in practice?

Notes

Patient-held records (PHRs) may become a reality in the NHS. Research has identified practical models which patients find acceptable and desirable. They feel more involved, better informed and it can improve co-ordination of care. They can correct errors in the record. They require the co-operation of all the medical practitioners involved in a patient's care and careful practice organisation to ensure PHRs are updated.

One model would involve the replacement of all practice written records with a practice computer record and a patient-held written or computer printed summary. More research is needed.

Question 2
- What do you find stressful about general practice?
- What is burnout?
- How would you avoid it in your professional life?

Notes

Burnout is a syndrome consisting of emotional exhaustion, depersonalization of others and a lack of personal accomplishment. It leads to diminished performance, fatigue and inefficiency. Stresses such as living with uncertainty, unforeseen errors, inappropriate demands, heartsink patients and unsociable hours require recognition. There is no association between age and burnout. Survival skills include good time-management, development of other interests, planning breaks, forming realistic goals and keeping your sense of humour.

Question 3
- You are asked to supervise a boxing match at the local boy's club. It will be cancelled unless you do it. Will you?
- Does the BMA have any opinions about this?
- How do you feel about going against the wishes of your union?

Notes

Justify your choice of answer. Will you let your own opinions on contact sport predominate? Be aware that the BMA has campaigned for some time for stricter legal regulation of boxing. It is the only sport where injury is a result of correct performance. Assault can be legal because of consent e.g. in the case of surgery, but some feel that standards are inadequate and that could leave a participating doctor open to be sued for negligence.

Question 4

- What techniques do you know for breaking upsetting news?
- What else can you do to make it easier?
- How does it affect you?

Notes

This question may be dressed up in a scenario making it easier to overlook the principles. Not all bad news is gravely bad but you must be sensitive to the impact on the patient. Be prepared, check what is known, fire a warning shot, and explain slowly and clearly. Allow the patient to respond and empathize. The use of contact, diagrams and tape recording the session to play back later can make a world of difference.

Question 5

- What do you understand by "morbidity registers"?
- What are the implications for running your practice?
- Will patient care improve as a result?

Notes

The change from the treatment of individuals to the management of populations requires increasingly well-kept registers of patients with particular medical conditions. All practice staff need to understand the purpose and importance of the registers and their commitment ensured to keep them up to date. A plan identifying sources of information and a programme for updating the register needs to be agreed. Population strategies and implementation of guidelines is difficult unless the relevant patients are found and given the opportunity of the latest recognized treatment. Audit will exact increasing standards and good practices will be required to illustrate performance.

VIVA TABLE 2

Question 1
- What makes consultations go wrong?
- How can you make sure patients understand what you tell them?
- What are the consequences of getting it wrong?

Notes

Poor consultation technique results in a poor doctor–patient relationship. Matters range from the simple such as the use of language on both sides of the consultation to more complex issues relating to underlying health beliefs which require time to explore. All are crucial to a good relationship and ensuring trust and compliance. Daily pressures and prejudices affect how we operate. Use of open posture, eye contact, an attentive pose and other techniques to feign interest help. Checking understanding and backing it up with written information helps. The effective GP must have a career-long dedication to minimize the many negative influences upon clear communication. Complaints and even more stress are the rewards for failure.

Question 2
- Why do you want to be a GP?
- What will you do if you do not feel you know enough?
- Why should you bother keeping up to date?

Notes

Rewarding aspects of practice include independence, holistic nature of care, the challenge of problem-solving, opportunity to work flexibly, continuity of care, status in society and financial rewards. Lifelong self-directed learning requires targeting of weak areas. These may be identified during everyday work or discussion groups to build up a personal development plan. Reading, listening to patients and teaching are all ways of identifying such areas. The GMC's Good Medical Practice requires you to keep your knowledge and skills up to date. Revalidation will incorporate aspects of an educational portfolio and the process should result in increased professional satisfaction.

Question 3
- A patient comes to see you asking you to recommend a cosmetic surgeon for breast enhancement. What are your feelings about this?
- What is the GP's role in this area?
- Does cosmetic surgery do any good psychologically?

Notes

In most areas, cosmetic surgery is not available on the NHS in the absence of significant psychological morbidity. Many now self-refer to clinics but some will approach their GP for advice on a safe approach. This gives an opportunity to explore underlying personal/relationship issues and discuss any risks and complications and encourage realistic expectations. If the decision to continue is made, a referral letter summarizing the patient's background will be of use. To help the patient choose a plastic surgeon, contacting the British Association of Aesthetic Plastic Surgeons identifies well qualified and experienced surgeons. The GMC also holds a record of qualified specialists who have undergone specialist training. A phone check can be done on a named surgeon. Some surgeons in cosmetic clinics may lack expertise.

Question 4
- Whose model of the consultation do you follow?
- How do you find someone's hidden agenda?
- What is meant by the "infinite potential" of the consultation?

Notes
Discuss your favourite model. For example, Pendleton's seven-point plan aims to define reasons for attendance, consider other problems, choose appropriate action with the patient, achieve shared understanding, involve patient in management and encourage to accept responsibility, use time and resources appropriately and establish or maintain a relationship to help achieve other tasks.

Question 5
- Mrs. Carr is an anxious patient of yours. She returns to see you a week after you visited her at home and prescribed penicillin for her tonsillitis. She says she is no better despite finishing the course and presents the empty bottle of tablets. The label says penicillamine instead of penicillin. She is otherwise well. What is your reaction?
- Do you tell her the truth?
- What is significant event analysis?

Notes
Horror! Informing her will be distressing for both parties although you have not yet confirmed whether the error is yours or the pharmacist's. A meeting with him is necessary. If the mistake was entirely trivial with no potential consequences, you may choose not to inform her but you do have a duty as a doctor to tell the truth especially as the drug is potentially toxic. You could only justify non-disclosure if you felt giving the information would be likely to cause serious harm to her mental health. A little anxiety does not qualify. You may face anger and distress but hopefully honesty will strengthen the doctor–patient relationship. A critical incident review should ensure that it does not happen again.

VIVA TABLE 3

Question 1
- How would you react to a request by a patient to see her notes?
- Are there any circumstances in which you would refuse?
- What if she disagrees with some of the non-medical facts and requests you change them?

Notes

It is useful to understand the reasons. A review of the notes may allow this to be ascertained. A written application is necessary and access made within 40 days. Third party information should be removed unless the third party gives consent. Since March 2000 as a result of The Data Protection Act 1998, the deadline for access to records of 1 November 1991 no longer applies. Patients are entitled to see all their manual and computer records in a read-able form and have a health professional explain anything not understood. Outright refusal can only take place if the release is believed to lead to the possibility of serious harm to the physical or mental health of any party. This decision can be challenged in the courts. Non-medical facts can be corrected but if they are believed accurate, the best approach is to add a comment about the patient's objection.

Question 2
- What are the problems with one patient consulting on behalf of another?
- How can you maintain confidentiality?
- What will be your approach to the consultation?

Notes

Third party consultations present difficult issues of ethics and confidentiality. The scenario (e.g. mother about daughter or wife about husband) will influence the specifics of your answer. Focus on the underlying reasons and try to identify which party needs most help. Is this a sign of disharmony in the relationship, a personal cry for help or genuine concern for the third party? Avoid a breach of confidentiality and act in the best interests of your patient. You may need to take steps to get permission to divulge information. Your main aim is to promote communication between the two parties.

Question 3
- How do patients put doctors at risk?
- How might doctors put their patients at risk?
- What steps will you take to avoid this throughout your career?

Notes

Doctors may inadvertently put patients at risk due to physical or mental illness, poor decision-making and lack of knowledge or competence. You can help to minimize this with efforts to optimize skills such as listening, identifying goals and giving information in a structured manner along with principles of lifelong learning e.g. from your own mistakes.

Question 4

- An 18 year old man presents a health report for you to fill out for the army. He asks you to omit the diagnosis of asthma that he was given at the age of 5 as he has not used inhalers for the last 7 years. What is your response?
- If you do not do as he asks he will be refused a chance in the army. You know his educational background is poor and unemployment in his peers is high. How does this affect your opinion?
- Would you ever lie for a patient?

Notes

You have an obligation to tell the truth or be open to litigation. The stress of a new physical challenge could provoke some of his previous symptoms. A doctor's signature must be a guarantee of probity.

Your patient is putting you in an unreasonable position and perhaps leaving you open to litigation and a claim of conspiracy to defraud and serious professional misconduct. The information is relevant and there is a moral right to reveal it. Full disclosure regarding the history of the illness and lack of symptoms is a safe approach and can allow the army's medical adviser to make an appropriate decision. Lack of honesty at this stage will not find favour with an employer.

The patient has a right to read the report before it is sent under the Access to Medical Records Act 1988. If the patient delivers the report there is even an opportunity to change it without your knowledge!

Question 5

- Do you agree to see pharmaceutical representatives?
- How do you view their promotional material?
- What would influence you to prescribe a new drug?

Notes

Drug reps can be seen the bearer of free pens (and a pleasant source of relief for a GP) or a pest. Research suggests they are still the source of much information on drugs for GPs but this information must be looked at carefully using the principles of critical appraisal. The developments that the companies finance bring an array of new advances to improve patient care. Doctors can be divided into innovators, moderators and procrastinators depending on their keenness to try new drugs. Factors which influence the confidence to use new drugs include cost, perceived benefit, presence of guidelines and use of the drugs by specialists.

VIVA TABLE 4

Question 1

- You receive a request for a statin from an insistent patient who does not fit the guidelines for treatment. How would this make you feel?
- Outline your approach.
- What if she perseveres?

Notes

Patients have access to a lot of information but can fail to apply it appropriately. She requires an understanding approach and reassurance that the benefit of the medication is not considered sufficient in her circumstances. Explanation of the underlying evidence for your decision and the lifelong commitment of treatment and side effects may help. There is no obligation to prescribe on demand and you may face criticism in the face of an adverse event. You are a gatekeeper for resources and it is not possible or desirable to treat everybody. It may initiate similar requests.

If you fail to reassure her, you would have to justify a decision to prescribe even if it was done as a private prescription which she would find expensive.

Question 2

- What do you feel when a patient brings you a list of problems to the consultation?
- Are there any ways to turn this to your advantage?
- What communication skills will help you here?

Notes

Admit your genuine feelings and recognize your frustrations. It is known that the majority of patients have more than one problem for each appointment. Learn to accept this. It can help to organize workload. Assume a list is present and listen carefully without interrupting initially. It is an important task to discover this list early in the consultation and prioritise it. Evidence shows that doctors interrupt their patients' opening statements after an average of 18 seconds. And that allowing continuation elicits more concerns. The first problem may not be the most important. Be alert for non-verbal clues and reflect these back. Ask early on "is there anything else?" and negotiate an agenda for the consultation. Seeking out problems will save time in the long run.

Question 3

- What are the strengths and weaknesses of practice-based learning?
- How does so-called evidence-based research help you learn?
- How will you avoid getting stale as a GP?

Notes

Practice-based learning can share knowledge and insights, allow effective use of resources and strengthen the team but other members of the primary health care team may not have the same educational needs. Plans must always be tailored. Methods of broadening your outlook include teaching, extra courses, clinical assistantships and A&E sessions.

Evidence provides a good framework for learning and better communication with patients but it cannot be applied crudely. Results cannot be extrapolated beyond the choice of research group and many outcomes cannot be measured.

Question 4

- What is gained by removing a patient from your list?
- What would make you remove a patient from your list?
- How would you try to prevent this arising?

Notes

The RCGP's guidance on removal of patients from the practice list justifies removal in three circumstances: (1) crime and deception e.g. deliberate lying to obtain benefit; (2) violence including verbal abuse; (3) distance e.g. moving out of designated practice area. In the event of irretrievable breakdown of the doctor–patient relationship, it also recommends a careful plan of communication with colleagues and patient, a review of contributory factors, and a succession of steps to be taken to remove the patient from the list.

Question 5

- A 15 year old girl comes to you and admits she is being sexually abused by her father. She is happy to talk to you about this but requests you tell no-one as she will be leaving for college soon. What is your reaction?
- Will you break her confidence?
- Where does your duty of care lie?

Notes

Believe her and listen sympathetically. She will need advice on pregnancy and sexually transmitted disease. Do you consider her to be competent under the Fraser ruling? You owe her a duty of confidentiality but have a duty of care to protect her from further abuse. You must decide if it is in her best interests to disclose to a child protection team. This is best done with her consent so make every effort. Failure to act on the information could be seen as condoning incest and child abuse. However, action may provoke a serious reaction such as running away. Other help such as counselling or sexual abuse helplines could be offered. As her GP you may well feel you need to discuss the situation with a specialist.

VIVA TABLE 5

Question 1
- If you become an employer (a GP partner), how will you get the most out of your staff?
- What is meant by staff appraisal?
- How might it affect the development of a group practice?

Notes

Staff appraisal is a widespread technique of continual review that allows review of employees' performance, goals and development. It allows a more informed relationship with the employer and clarification of duties as well as identifying problem areas and training needs. It is done in protected time and forms are available to give structure to the session. Most of all it is an opportunity to give praise. A smile and a thank-you are invaluable. Use them liberally.

Question 2
- Do you think GPs should be involved with research?
- Where might you get help for an interesting research project in general practice?
- What are the implications of doing research on patients in practice?

Notes

Developing an interest in research is a healthy part of the learning process for the interested GP. Practical help and funding can be accessed via your clinical tutor, post-graduate professor and from local research groups and centrally from the RCGP. The National Group on Research and Development in Primary Care has been criticized as not being sufficiently clinical concentrating mainly on issues of organization and GP attitudes.

Question 3
- Why do patients come to see a doctor?
- Why do some patients consult frequently for trivial complaints?
- What strategies do you think can tackle this?

Notes

Patients can approach a GP for many reasons e.g. need for treatment/reassurance, under pressure from relatives, attention-seeking, low level of personal responsibility and legitimization of sickness.

Frequent attendance can represent inability to cope, poor home support, an unresolved agenda, an underlying undiagnosed problem, inappropriate health beliefs and unrealistic expectations. Doctors require good communication skills to find out which. Practices can arrange a meeting to broach the problem with strategies such as firm (rather than opportunistic) arrangements for review, agreeing to avoid unnecessary prescribing or giving too much time which may confirm the patient's expectations. A sympathetic approach incorporating the patient's own health beliefs can give confidence for self-management. Resources such as self-help groups, day centres or anxiety-management courses may have a role.

Question 4

- What do you understand by clinical governance?
- What is the Commission for Health Improvement?
- How does the work of NICE affect your practice?

Notes

Clinical governance is the initiative of the White Paper, The New NHS: Modern and Dependable. Its agenda is quality. It involves action to avoid risks, investigate adverse situations and disseminate the lessons learned. It advocates systems that ensure continuous evolution of clinical care at local level throughout the NHS. It is a framework to improve patient care through a commitment to high standards and personal and team development. It covers a wide range of areas from identifying poor performance and unacceptable variations in care to promoting lifelong learning and personal accreditation. It advocates the development of cost-effective, evidence-based clinical practice in an accountable and transparent system. The Commission for Health Improvement will oversee the quality of clinical governance and of services and visits each PCG every 4 years.

The National Institute of Clinical Excellence appraises evidence and produces and disseminates clinical guidelines to promote cost-effective therapies and uniform clinical standards.

Question 5

- How can you assess quality in general practice?
- What is the role of the college in this?
- How can PACT data help?

Notes

Many variables have been used. The RCGP has taken a central role in this and its document Recognising Quality of Care in General Practice describes these. Components of quality include professional performance (technical quality), use of resources (efficiency), risk-management and patient satisfaction. Single performance indicators are a crude and inaccurate assessment of quality e.g. referral rates – does a good doctor refer more or fewer patients? Prescribing patterns (as shown in the Prescribing Analysis and Cost data) are not a good index of overall quality of GPs. Indeed achieving a performance indicator can replace the pursuit of high quality care.

Quality is indicated by the likes of vocational training, possession of the MRCGP and Fellowship by Assessment and the Quality Practice Awards. Practice and personal development plans continue this trend. Measuring quality requires a countrywide, multi-dimensional framework covering all areas of general practice including clinical audit. It may be that at least initially quality markers need to be set at different levels and standards to stimulate and encourage GPs who are on different points on the quality continuum.

VIVA TABLE 6

Question 1
- A mother comes to the surgery and says she is certain that her husband is going to take her daughter out of the country to have her circumcised. She is desperate for help, what is your advice?
- Whom might you approach for advice?
- What might a social services referral achieve?

Notes
The Prohibition of Circumcision Act 1989 makes this procedure an offence except in specific physical or mental grounds. It is child abuse and your duty is to safeguard the child's welfare. A Child Protection Investigation involving social services should take place. The aim is to clarify the facts, identify areas of (grounds for) concern, look for evidence to suspect the child is at risk of significant harm and decide on where the child will be safe. It will involve a multidisciplinary team with sensitive communication skills in an open and honest discussion with all the relevant parties.

Question 2
- How can you avoid complaints?
- What action should be taken to deal with a complaint to the practice?
- What are the possible outcomes of a complaint?

Notes
A story always has two sides and frequently a breakdown of communication is to blame for complaints. The GMC requires you to give a prompt cordial and full explanation of what went wrong with an apology if appropriate. The vast majority of complaints can be dealt with by an in-house complaints procedure. This delegates the initial action usually to the practice manager, requires contact with the complainant within two working days and facilitates appropriate investigation and action. A full response should be made within 10 working days. Outcomes include referral to the health authority which may result in independent review, referral for conciliation, referral back to the practice or advice on approaching the Health Service Commissioner (Ombudsman) who can recommend a discipline committee investigation, refer to the GMC or to an NHS tribunal.

Question 3
- Flexible ways of working such as part-time, locum or job-shares are on the increase. What impact do you think that growing trend will have?
- Would you prefer to work as a locum or a principal?
- How would you prevent isolation as a locum?

Notes
There may be fewer partners to share the out-of-hours service or attend practice meetings. Voting rights may need discussing in the case of job-sharing principals. There is more to being a GP than coming in for two or three surgeries a week. Communication and continuity of care is further eroded.

On the other hand it may give an opportunity to increase the range of services a practice offers.

Implications for the doctor are positive. Many feel the loss of earnings is more than outweighed by the improvements in lifestyle. Other interests, medical and non-medical can be taken up. Stress is less and part-timers show a lower rate of burnout.

The National Association of Non-Principals and regional locum groups such as the North East Locum Group give a voice to the growing number of flexible workers and help outline the requirements of the locum doctor.

Question 4

- What makes you bring a patient back for review?
- Why might one partner consistently run his surgeries later than another?
- How might this be tackled in practice?

Notes

Review can be doctor-initiated or patient-initiated. It can represent lack of confidence, a need for emotional involvement or even to impress a patient. The passage of time is needed to make many diagnoses and review of progress is part of good care. Stabilizing a chronic condition, offering psychological support all take time. Regular appointments may also reduce the need for emergency appointments in some patients. Appointments can get blocked and one doctor consistently being booked well in advance can cause practice tensions. This may be due to different expertise and case-mix. A practice meeting can air the issue. Solutions include a change in the doctor's habits, adoption of personal lists or introduction of a catch-up break to the surgery.

Question 5

- How might a system of central electronic records with multiple points of access work in practice?
- Do shared-access records pose a threat to confidentiality?
- Who do you think should have access?

Notes

Pilots are in progress for an integrated care records service – ICRS. Records held by the Primary Care Trust are updated from areas of service provision. The GP updates his own notes which update the PCT record automatically. District, community and school nurses may access and update records and it is expected that hospital and out-of-hours services will too. The many people with access to someone's most personal information is a concern for confidentiality issues. The process is far less protected from hackers. Who has the legal responsibility for the data – the PCT?

VIVA TABLE 7

Question 1
- What is the LMC?
- What is the GMSC?
- Would you be interested in becoming a member later on in your career?

Notes

The local medical committee (LMC) is a group of peer-elected GPs and the only true representative body of GPs working in a particular area. Members are appointed to various committees of the health authority e.g. new health promotion activities. There is an elected chairman.

The General Medical Services Committee (GMSC) consists of GP members elected by several LMCs and is the sole representative of all GPs in the country. It is the executive at the annual conference of LMCs. Although technically a standing committee of the BMA, membership is not a requirement. It connects the voice of local representatives to the negotiating sub-committees of the Department of Health.

Question 2
- What does the term heartsink mean to you?
- Can you think of any in your practice?
- Can you identify what sort of groups they fall into?

Notes

"Heartsinks" are demanding patients who consult frequently and invoke feelings of despair, anger and frustration in the primary health care team. They are typically female, over 40, demanding, frequent attenders who lack insight and suffer with a high degree of anxiety/depression. Their locus of control empowers their GP as "the powerful other", believing that the doctor is in charge of their health. Models have identified four categories – the dependent clinger, the entitled demander, the manipulative help-rejecter and the self-destructive denier (Groves, 1951).

Question 3
- What does the Royal College of General Practitioners do?
- Why do you want to be a member?
- What can you offer the college?

Notes

The work of the college includes development of policy and clinical guidelines, raising standards and quality in primary health care, providing education and training, facilitation of research, producing publications, encouraging recruitment and influencing government policy.

It produces a dedicated journal, has a comprehensive information service and advances GP-led training. It enables access to becoming a trainer or a fellow and connects like-minded people in encouraging positive aspects of practice. On the other hand the journal has been widely criticized as dull and lacking usefulness and there is a lack of devolved regional power. After achieving the standard, there are probably few immediate advantages for the new principal. (This would be a brave approach to take in the exam!)

Question 4

- What does the practice nurse do in your practice?
- Would you rather employ a nurse practitioner or a practice nurse?
- How do you see their roles developing in the future?

Notes

Practice nurses are valuable members of the primary care health team. Their interests and abilities enable extension of their nursing role to other duties such as pill checks, chronic disease management, HRT clinics, assisting minor surgery and advice on health education. Nurse practitioners are a much more expensive resource with major implications for training and protocol development for the practice. They may be a triage resource or run their own lists. They see about half as many patients per hour as a doctor and their competence must be guaranteed by the supervising GP. Their lack of knowledge of physiology, pharmacology, lack of experience in taking responsibility for therapy as well as lack of prescribing powers limits their role.

Question 5

- How do patients get most of their information?
- What are patient participation groups?
- How can they help the practice?

Notes

Many sources inform patients nowadays. These include doctors, other health professionals, pharmacists, family, friends, self-help groups, product inserts within medication, information leaflets, radio, television, newspaper magazines and the Internet. Much of it varies in quality and relevance to the individual.

Patient participation groups are patient representatives who can liaise with a nominated GP and cover various roles. They may help deal with complaints, administer donations, aid awareness of services for patients, aid planning of developments and identify unmet needs. Liaison with the lay member of the primary care group better represents views.

VIVA TABLE 8

Question 1
- Do you think cannabis should be prescribable?
- Many would disagree with you – what do you think concerns them?
- Do you think the BMA would support legalization?

Notes
Cannabinoids appear to have use as a treatment for symptoms such as pain, insomnia, helping opiate withdrawal and AIDS-related problems. No deaths have been attributed to it alone but rigorous pharmaceutical research with randomized controlled trials are needed. Further work will help identify the useful cannabinoids. The BMA produced a book on the Therapeutic Uses of Cannabis in 1997. Options of limited prescribability through to the consequences of legalization may be discussed.

Question 2
- How do you filter through the sources of information that a GP receives each week?
- What article has changed your practice?
- How would you organize your practice to make sure nothing important is missed?

Notes
Identify the factors of a publication which make it interesting and relevant to you. You will need to develop strategies to keep on top of developments in a time-efficient way. You may choose to concentrate on a few sources, maintain a questioning approach, and read to remember e.g. by highlighting key facts and having a reference to articles you keep. The value of articles written by GPs could be discussed.

The importance of practice failsafes cannot be overstated.

Question 3
- You spend 15 minutes performing an elderly driving medical on a 77 year old man. The findings are satisfactory. You present him with a bill for the BMA recommended fee. He says it was done the previous time by your partner for free. What are your feelings about this?
- What implications are there for the practice?
- How will you prevent this happening again?

Notes
After spending your time on this you are bound to feel irritation. Recognize it and step back. Clearly the patient should have been warned to expect the bill. Your partner's activities should be discussed as it has impact on the rest of the practice and he is partly responsible for jeopardising your doctor–patient relationship. The practice policy should be clarified. A suitable way to leave this may be to verify your personal policy and leave the form for collection on payment of the required fee.

Question 4

- A patient approaches you to ask you to prescribe the new drug that prevents heart disease. He brings a newspaper cutting with him. How would this make you feel?
- What beliefs may underlie this request?
- Pretend I am that patient. What do you say to me?

Notes

This is not an uncommon scenario for the GP. You need to avoid feeling threatened. Listen to the patient's views and read the article. Understanding his expectations is essential to a good approach. Be ready for a little role-play.

You may choose to admit your ignorance of the drug, discuss your opinion of the validity of the claims and the way you prescribe medicines e.g. according to guidelines or after proof of value. He should not leave feeling that you are closed to new ideas or only looking after your budget.

Question 5

- A 72 year old lady comes to see you following the death of her husband after 3 weeks on a life support machine. She is certain he would have abhorred this and has come to tell you that she would not want this treatment in similar circumstances. How can you help her?
- Is an advance directive legally binding in the UK?
- What advice would you give to a patient who was thinking about writing one?

Notes

Advance directives (or living wills) ensure the wishes of a competent patient are considered when informed consent can no longer be obtained. Their legal basis is in case law rather than statutory law. It requires a patient to be fully informed which presents problems with generalized directives as any doubt in intention favours medical intervention. Problems can be minimized by mentioning specific scenarios, reviewing every 5 years and by having the patient inform her relatives. Clear directives are as legally binding as any current decision by a competent patient. The GP's role is one of advisor and repository. Forms are available from the Euthanasia Society or the Terence Higgins Trust. Further guidance is available from the BMA Ethics Division.

VIVA TABLE 9

Question 1

- How should your consultation skills be checked throughout your career?
- What are your opinions on the use of video to assess consultation skills?
- What makes an "unacceptable GP"?

Notes

The quality of consultations will be a key feature of revalidation. The RCGP's document Good Medical Practice for GPs spells out the attributes of an "excellent GP" and the "unacceptable GP" who has poor communication and professional skills and provides a service that does not incorporate adequate consideration of patients' needs. Patient questionnaires and video are examples of methods of offering evidence of a high standard of care.

Question 2

- Your practice nurse gives advice that is incorrect. The patient complains. What do you do?
- What is the legal situation – is it your fault?
- What are you going to do to avoid it happening again?

Notes

The practice complaints procedure is required to process the complaint.

Practice nurses are professionals with their own insurance but as her employer you must provide adequate training, assessment and review of any problems.

You must do everything you can to prevent a recurrence and document it. Interview the nurse – there are two sides to every story. Review policies and protocols as necessary. Options for change may include the need for retraining, a revision of policy or creation of new guidelines.

Question 3

- How do you feel when running late?
- What would you do if you consistently felt that way?
- What could help you to organize your day?

Notes

Assess the demand of unscheduled tasks and your behaviour at work. Make sure tasks are prioritised. If it does not need doing, do not do it! Allow for delays in your schedule, set realistic targets in manageable chunks, have a systematic approach, learn to say no, delegate where you can and allow time for yourself every day.

Question 4

- After referring a 20 year old woman for a termination of pregnancy, she requests that you omit the incident from her notes. What issues does this raise for you?
- Will you agree to this request?
- Are there any circumstances in which you would change your mind?

Notes

You can approach this question as you would a written answer. Explore the reasons for her request and remind her of total confidentiality. You may or may not agree to her request but you will need to justify your answer in the face of challenge from the examiner. Records may be needed for any future health problems. Incomplete notes may prejudice future management in the event of complications. Your terms of service require you to keep adequate records for the current episode and any future events. They will help if the patient sees a different doctor next time and increase the awareness of possible psychological consequences. They are important in demonstrating a good standard of care. The GMC's Duties of a Doctor include a duty to make and keep proper records. Some omissions at the patient's request may have the intention of misleading for example a life assurance company. Omission in this context could result in an allegation of negligence against the GP.

Question 5

- Do you consider yourself a family doctor?
- Do you feel that home visits are a thing of the past to the modern GP?
- What might be the advantages of home visits?

Notes

Despite the decreasing trend, home visits are not going to go away. There remains a requirement for them within our terms of service and there are times when they can help you provide an improved and holistic standard of care. A home visit can allow a functional assessment of the patient in their own environment, help identify hazards, see the impact on the household and yield the opportunity to check compliance. They can reaffirm your role as a family doctor both to the patient and to you.

VIVA TABLE 10

Question 1

- What are your feelings about nurse prescribing?
- Have you ever asked a nurse's advice on what to prescribe?
- Do you feel prescribing powers should be extended to pharmacists?

Notes

Prescribing is a reality of modern health care for district nurses and health visitors and expansion of this is advocated by the government. Their experience with dressings and bandaging for example usually exceeds that of doctors. Use of a formulary is important. A distinction between dependent (treatment following doctor diagnosis) and independent (diagnosis and treatment) prescribing is important.

Question 2

- You are called by a patient complaining of severe headache who says she is unable to contact her own GP. What would your feelings be?
- How would you act?
- How close is the relationship between a GP and his colleagues in the same area?

Notes

Recognize the irritation that this problem will cause and be aware of the possibility of manipulation by the patient. You may be able to contact her own GP or if there is evidence of severe morbidity call an ambulance on her behalf.

The possibility of a serious diagnosis may compel you to visit. You will need to keep good records in the event of any future complaint.

The least you must do is assess need, act appropriately and inform the patient's GP.

Question 3

- The wife of a patient with terminal cancer comes to you asking for a sick note so that she can stay at home to look after him. She is generally well. What is your reaction?
- Would you consider such an action dishonest?
- Who would you ask for further help on this issue?

Notes

You may feel that documentation of the wife's distress at this unfortunate situation will enable you to sign a sick note. What you write on the sick note can be sufficiently vague e.g. stress-related problem. A less controversial approach would be to volunteer to write to the employer on the patient's behalf if you both felt this would be useful. Alternative strategies may involve offering extra help at home. A sick note renders a patient incapable of work. If no appropriate medical condition exists, supplying a certificate can be seen as clear dishonesty. Your defence union may not have a great deal of sympathy. The "family-friendly policies" of the Employment Relations Bill 1999 may be of use to facilitate unpaid leave.

226   *PRACTICE VIVAS*

Question 4

- You diagnose a viral infection in a 9 month baby. You spend time explaining the diagnosis and prescribe paracetamol but after the mother and baby leave, your receptionist comes to tell you that she wants to see another doctor. How do you feel?
- What options do you have?
- What factors might have influenced her behaviour?

Notes

Initially you may both feel anger. Clearly her expectations have not been met and her anxieties not relieved. Refusal of a second opinion will not help anybody. You may decide to offer to see her again if this is acceptable. A later appointment with a colleague will at least avoid an attendance at A&E or a possible night visit. Discussion with the relevant partner will make sure you are all singing from the same hymn sheet while allowing for the possibility of a diagnosis overlooked.

Question 5

- How important is a good receptionist to a practice?
- Do they have a role in triage?
- How would we audit the work they do?

Notes

A good receptionist is a priceless asset. They are the interface and first point of contact with the practice either by phone or in person. A good use of common sense allows them to help patients prioritize their appointments. A system needs to be in place which avoids them making decisions outside of their competence. Doctors need to be sufficiently accessible during surgery time to deal with any problems.

The GP must decide what tasks to delegate to the receptionist and provide adequate training.

FURTHER VIVA PRACTICE

VIVA 1

- Do you ever prescribe antibiotics over the phone?
- What are the dangers of doing so?
- How could you justify doing so in the event of a significant reaction?

- What is narrative-based medicine?
- How does it compare to a patient-centred or biomedical approach?
- Do you think that storytelling skills could help GPs communicate?

- Tell me about something interesting you have read recently.
- How do you know what you don't know?
- How would you get some objectivity into your personal development plan?

- When do you use private prescriptions?
- When do you refer patients privately?
- Would you consider becoming a private GP?

- You overhear your staff openly discussing the case history of one of your patients. How do you react?
- What efforts do you take in your practice to ensure confidentiality?
- What do you understand by the term "informed consent"?

VIVA 2

- Your partner refuses to give contraception or advice about terminations. What problems does this raise for the practice?
- You receive a complaint from a patient's participation group. How do you react?
- Do your personal feelings affect the way you perform as a GP?

- How do you prefer to learn?
- How does the Internet aid your PDP?
- How might you measure your professional achievements and shortcomings in five years time?

- Do you think there is any value in self-help groups?
- How would you react if you were asked to talk to the multiple sclerosis self-help group about the latest treatments?
- Do you ever suggest that your patients contact one of these groups? Why/Why not?

- Do you manage your time well?
- Have you mastered the art of delegation?
- You have a cold – are you coming into work today?

- What difficulties do you think your practice nurse faces in her job?
- What about the receptionists?
- How can you make sure these problems are recognized and try to improve communication in the primary health care team?

VIVA 3

- What do patients want from their GP?
- Are you aware of any legislation that has increased patients' expectations?
- A patient comes to you for anti-dandruff shampoo as it is cheaper on prescription. How do you feel about this use of resources?

- What techniques of consultation do you prefer?
- How do you assess your success?
- Persuade me to do more exercise.

- A patient has borrowed some omeprazole from a friend and found it has worked wonders for his dyspepsia. He comes to you for some more. How do you start the consultation?
- What are the issues this raises?
- How do you educate patients?

- How has computerization affected general practice?
- Would you communicate with your patients by email?
- Would you ever give them your home phone number?

- When you are a principal what piece of equipment would you most like that you have not got now?
- How will you convince me as your partner?
- How might it be financed?

VIVA 4

- Your next patient has been asked to attend after a severely dyskaryotic cervical smear result taken 8 months ago appears not to have been acted on. How would you have planned for this?
- How are you going to make sure she takes in what you say?
- How do you end the consultation?

- Your next patient has missed their last four appointments. What problems does this cause?
- How will you try to help the problem?
- What could the practice do as a group?

- You see one of your patients who has just been diagnosed with epilepsy driving down the high street. What action do you take?
- How can you progress without breaking confidentiality?
- Can you enlist anybody to help you?

- Why do people consult alternative practitioners?
- A patient of yours asks you to recommend a homeopath. How do you reply?
- She then asks your opinion on having Botox. How do you advise?

- What piece of litigation would you like to see to improve the standard of health care?
- What if there was no extra money available?
- How would you help promote a Give Up Smoking campaign?

- What book would you recommend a friend who wishes to pass the MRCGP? (No pressure!)
- What non-medical book would you recommend?
- How will you manage family life and life as a GP?

- Would you ever break the confidence of the patient?
- Would you inform a surgeon about the HIV positive status of a patient you are referring for hernia repair?
- How would you go about this?

- What do you think varies the rate of referral between GPs and between practices?
- Do you think this could be used as a marker of quality?
- Would you be happy to have your practice data published in a league table?

- During a minor surgery procedure, you discover you have accidentally injected a small amount of lignocaine with adrenaline into someone's finger. Do you admit the mistake?
- The amount is only very small and there will almost certainly be no after-effects. How do you react now?
- What are the consequences of each approach? Is total honesty always the best policy?

- You see one of your partners at a restaurant with the practice manager. Would this concern you?
- Would you tell anyone?
- How might it compromise the team?

- What is happening to the profession at the moment?
- How much of our work should be in disease prevention?
- Should we not focus more on disease management?

- An 80 year old lady with severe arthritis asks you to explain how many of her phenobarbitone tablets she would need to take in order to kill herself. What issues does this raise?
- How would you decide what to tell her?
- She is found the next day dead in bed. The family are against a post-mortem. Would you inform the coroner?

- You are telephoned by the police to attend a violent patient. How will you prepare yourself?
- What issues does this raise?
- What measures could you take to improve your safety at work?

- A lady who is the sole carer of her increasingly dependent mother says she is getting too much for her and tells you "you'll have to put her in a home!". How does this make you feel?
- Who is the patient here?
- What options can you suggest?

- You receive a call from a nursing home regarding a resident who has fallen out of bed and has pain in the leg. She asks if you want to visit or if she should just call an ambulance. What is your reply?
- Have you ever told a patient to go to A&E when you could have seen them yourself?
- How should a GP communicate with an A&E department?

VIVA 7

- You notice that one of your partners is becoming increasingly irritable and smelling of alcohol. You know that he is going through a divorce. How will you react?
- You feel that he is making mistakes. What will you do?
- Your health visitor comes to tell you that several mothers have complained he has alcohol on his breath. How do you respond?

- A patient asks for a repeat prescription for his father who is now living in Pakistan. Where does your clinical responsibility lie?
- Where would you go for further advice?
- What other options could you suggest?

- A newly registered patient comes to tell you he takes 100 mg of diazepam a day. He demands a 4 week supply. What do you say to him?
- How can you get more information?
- How will you formulate a plan of care?

- What do your patients need from you?
- What makes patients angry?
- Have you ever treated an angry patient?

- How would you assess your consultation skills?
- What does it mean to be a gatekeeper?
- How do financial limitations affect your day-to-day practice?

- It could be said that modern society is becoming deskilled at handling minor illness. Why do you think that is?
- What would you do to change it?
- How would you aim to redefine the term "minor illness"?

- How would you explain the diagnosis of asthma to the mother of a wheezing 3 year old?
- How do you find her level of understanding?
- How would you close the consultation?

- How well do you personally work in a team?
- What are your strengths and weaknesses?
- What situations in practice challenge your personal values and effectiveness as a doctor?

- How would you decide whether your primary care team is effective or not?
- What outcome measures would you like to target?
- Patients are crucial to our effectiveness, why do we not include them in our teams?

- How is the profession policed?
- How will you cope with pressure of a complaint?
- How will you approach the future in the face of increasing litigation and complaints?

VIVA 9

- Do you think the practice should have an ECG?
- Would you carry a defibrillator?
- What are the differences between rural and urban practice?

- What audit have you been involved in recently?
- Did it change practice?
- How would you choose an area of your practice to audit?

- How can you assess the needs of your patients and respond to them?
- What would you do if someone asked you to prescribe a tonic?
- Would you prescribe vitamin supplements?

- What is telemedicine?
- How can technological developments improve patient care?
- How do you see the work of the GP in 20 years time?

- You receive a telephone call from the local pharmacist saying that the prescription you gave to your previous patient has the wrong name on it. What is your reaction?
- How can you avoid such mistakes happpening?
- How might this affect your relationship with staff and patients?

- You get to the end of the day and realize you forgot to go on one of your visits at lunchtime?
- How do you feel?
- How would you prevent this in future?

- You are asked to give a talk on improving health care in areas of poverty. How would you prepare?
- What measures of deprivation do you know?
- How would you increase your awareness of your patients' problems throughout your career?

- What difficulties does having doctors as your patients present?
- What is mentorship?
- Do you ever prescribe medicines without clear evidence of their benefit?

- You meet one of your patients in the street. Would you ask her how she is?
- Are you prepared to be always on duty?
- How might your answer affect you and those around you?

- You become aware that an HIV patient of yours has not informed his partner of his status. Where does your duty of care lie?
- His partner comes to see you for advice on starting a family. What will you say?
- Would you be happy to breach confidentiality?

FURTHER DILEMMAS TO CONSIDER

1. A retired 75 year old patient of yours asks you for a certificate to say he is fit to learn to scuba dive on holiday.
2. A man is visited in the night by the deputizing service. He is given amoxicillin despite telling the doctor about his penicillin allergy. He sees you the following day with a severe rash consistent with his allergy.
3. A terminally ill patient requests help to end his life.
4. A consultant asks you to prescribe a treatment that he cannot afford to on his budget.
5. What sort of procedures do you think should be outside the scope of the NHS due to budget constraints?
6. A 40 year old patient asks you to refer him for reversal of vasectomy.
7. A 20 year old epileptic comes to see you with the good news that she has had no fits for a year and has stopped her medication.
8. You receive a request to visit a lady who has suffered miscarriage 2 days ago.
9. A patient asks you to release his notes to a nearby private GP.
10. A pharmacist calls to check a prescription for 200 codeine tablets that you have signed. He believes that it has been altered and you do recall prescribing only 20 tablets.
11. A patient requests a second opinion that you do not believe to be necessary.
12. A patient is abusive to staff.
13. You receive two complaints regarding one of your receptionists.
14. A patient with chronic renal failure tells you he is no longer willing to submit to dialysis.
15. A partner suggests that you should provide an evening clinic for the many people who find difficulty getting to the surgery.
16. A mother phones after finding her 5 month old baby apparently dead.
17. A 16 year old girl in the middle of her GCSEs presents with a sore throat requesting antibiotics.
18. A moribund terminal care patient looked after by visits from yourself and a practice nurse lives with a caring wife and son. On attending, you find his syringe driver which had nearly 20 hours to run is empty. The patient is dead.
19. A mother of a 14 year old girl you have recently started on the pill asks to see her daughter's notes.
20. A patient has returned from a specialist with a diagnosis of retrobulbar neuritis. He comes to you to clarify things. He was told he has some inflammation of the nerve behind the eye which has settled now.
21. You are asked to provide a sip-feed (a borderline substance) for a nursing home resident.
22. A 26 year old lawyer considering pregnancy comes to request immunization against chickenpox.
23. A private GP clinic is set up locally offering 24 hour care including telephone consults and home visits.

24. You see a man whom you have certified sick with back pain for the past 3 months building a garden wall.

25. A patient with rhinitis has not responded to treatment. She requests referral to a distant clinical ecology consultant for food allergy.

APPENDIX 1

APPRAISING THE ARTICLE

This checklist of questions to ask yourself is a useful way of analysing clinical papers. Comments can be made on each point in a positive or negative vein to create an answer with structure.

Introduction
- Are the aims stated clearly?
- Does the study match up to the aims?
- Is literature reviewed to place the article in perspective?

Method
- What is the study design? e.g. qualitative/quantitative, observational/experimental, retrospective/prospective, longitudinal/cross-sectional.
- Is the study design appropriate?
- Is there a gold standard for comparison?
- Do the instruments have validity in practice? e.g. are questions designed to avoid bias and ambiguity?
- Are the inclusion (and exclusion) criteria clear?
- Is the population representative of a GP population? e.g. similar age–sex distribution.
- Is power calculated and the sample size sufficient for significance?
- Is the sample unchanged during the study?
- Are the controls appropriate?
- Is the method of randomization described sufficient to allow reproduction of the experiment? Is it fair?
- Is the time-span defined and appropriate?
- Is treatment clear?
- Are outcome criteria clearly defined?
- Are the end-points soft or hard? Are they appropriate?
- Are all relevant outcomes included?
- Is it truly blind to patients and clinicians?

Results
- Is the response rate reasonable? (above 70% is good).
- Is follow-up adequate?
- Are all subjects accounted for? e.g. is analysis by intention to treat and are drop-outs adequately explained?
- Are data represented honestly with tables and graphs?
- Are statistics appropriate for all the findings?
- Do they include confidence limits and p values?

Discussion

- Were the aims met?
- Is there an objective discussion of limitations and applicability?
- Are conclusions justified and speculations realistic?
- Is there comparison with previous research?

Overall

- Was the study clear, valid, ethical and worthwhile?
- Are the conclusions affordable, available and sensible enough to bring about a change in practice?

APPENDIX 2

REVISED KEY TO GRADING OF EVIDENCE STATEMENTS AND GRADING OF RECOMMENDATIONS

Hierarchy of study types
- Systematic reviews and meta-analyses of randomized controlled trials.
- Randomized controlled trials.
- Non-randomized intervention studies.
- Observational studies.
- Non-experimental studies.
- Expert opinion.

Revised grading system for recommendations in evidence-based guidelines

Levels of evidence:

1++ High quality meta-analyses, systematic reviews of RCTs, or RCTs with a very low risk of bias.

1+ Well conducted meta-analyses, systematic reviews of RCTs, or RCTs with a low risk of bias.

1 Meta-analyses, systematic reviews of RCTs, or RCTs with a high risk of bias.

2++ High quality systematic reviews of case–control or cohort studies or high quality case–control or cohort studies with a very low risk of confounding, bias, or chance and a high probability that the relationship is causal.

2+ Well conducted case–control or cohort studies with a low risk of confounding, bias, or chance and a moderate probability that the relationship is causal.

2 Case–control or cohort studies with a high risk of confounding, bias, or chance and a significant risk that the relationship is not causal.

3 Non-analytic studies, e.g. case reports, case series.

4 Expert opinion.

Grades of recommendations:

A At least one meta-analysis, systematic review, or RCT rated as 1++ and directly applicable to the target population or a systematic review of RCTs or a body of evidence consisting principally of studies rated as 1+ directly applicable to the target population and demonstrating overall consistency of results

B A body of evidence including studies rated as 2++ directly applicable to the target population and demonstrating overall consistency of results or extrapolated evidence from studies rated as 1++ or 1+

C A body of evidence including studies rated as 2+ directly applicable to the target population and demonstrating overall consistency of results or extrapolated evidence from studies rated as 2++

D Evidence level 3 or 4 *or* extrapolated evidence from studies rated as 2+

REFERENCE

A new system for grading recommendations in evidence based guidelines. Harbour,
R and Miller, J SIGN *BMJ* **323:** 334–336, 2001.

APPENDIX 3

HOT TOPICS

This list may be a useful starting point to identify topics of value but does not claim to be comprehensive. Keeping up to date is essential to identify current key topics in general practice.

Clinical management
- Alcohol and drugs.
- Aspirin/anticoagulation .
- Asthma.
- Atrial fibrillation.
- Back pain.
- Breast disease and screening protocols.
- Care of the elderly.
- Chlamydia.
- COPD.
- Coronary heart disease.
- Dementia.
- Depression and the role of the GP.
- Diabetic care.
- Domiciliary thrombolysis.
- Epilepsy.
- Heart failure.
- *Helicobacter pylori*.
- Home birth.
- Homeopathy.
- HRT.
- Hyperlipidaemia and statins.
- Hypertension.
- Genetic counselling.
- Minor illness e.g. sore throat and otitis media.
- Obesity.
- Schizophrenia.
- Smoking cessation.
- Stroke management.

Administrative areas
- Advance directives.
- Complaints procedures.
- Consultation techniques.
- Confidentiality and HIV.
- Extended roles.
- Health promotion including sexual health.
- Information systems.
- Informed consent.

- MMR controversy.
- New contract and initiatives in primary care.
- National Service Frameworks.
- NICE.
- Open access to services.
- Out-of-hours work patterns.
- Poverty and deprivation.
- Practice formularies.
- Rationing.
- Reaccreditation.
- Refugees and asylum seekers.
- Role of counsellors.
- Salaried doctors.
- Screening controversies e.g. prostate, bowel cancer.
- Stress and burnout.
- Walk-in centres and NHS Direct.

INDEX

Palliative care 20, 64
Parkinson's disease 176
Paternity test 202
Patient-held records 208
Peripheral arterial disease 28
Pharmacists 36, 53
Physician's assistant 140
Poverty 19, 100
Practice nurses 152, 221, 224
Practice website 118, 139
Prescribing 74, 156, 226
Prescribing formulary 78

Quality 127, 217

Rationing 22
Receptionists 227
Refugees 18
Research 216
Risk 212

Schizophrenia 182
Screening 52, 662, 95, 142, 146, 198
Self-diagnosis 48

Self-harm 70
Smoking 28, 87, 159, 174
Soiling 112
Solo GP 46
Somatisation 91
Sore throat 38
Spirometry 172
Statins 27, 28, 135, 166, 214
Stress 54, 208
Stroke 166

Telephone 102, 170
Terminal care 20, 64
Temination of pregnancy 7, 225
Thrombolysis 34

UTI 196

Vaccination 160, 162
Violence 9, 18, 58, 180

Walk-in centres 68
Wilson's criteria 62